ౙ౦ల ౖ౦ౖ

JUST THINK,
I Could Have Been Normal

ᖀౖ౦ ౖ౦ᖂ

Growing Up *Extraordinary* with Cerebral Palsy

Nova Bannatyne-Eng

Edited by
George Vernon William Kruse

Agio
PUBLISHING HOUSE

151 Howe Street, Victoria BC Canada V8V 4K5

Photos from the private collection of the author
unless otherwise noted.

Permission to quote his poem *A Prisoner of Dependence*
was graciously provided by poet Richard A. Watson.

Just Think, I Could Have Been Normal
ISBN 978-1-927755-40-2 (paperback)
ISBN 978-1-927755-41-9 (ebook)
Cataloguing information available from
Library and Archives Canada.

Printed on acid-free paper.

Agio Publishing House is a socially responsible enterprise,
measuring success on a triple-bottom-line basis.

10 9 8 7 6 5 4 3 2 1.2

DEDICATION

This book is dedicated
to my family.

ৎ৹৹ ৹৹৹

PREFACE

৹৹৹ ৹৹৹

Nova Bannatyne-Eng was born with cerebral palsy (CP), brain damage due to a lack of oxygen. She was never expected to walk or talk or live a full life amongst 'normal' children. However, she proved many people wrong.

Born in 1956 and raised in Kimberley, BC, Nova was one of the first students with a significant disability to be integrated into and graduate from public school in British Columbia. This autobiography, *Just Think, I Could Have Been Normal*, documents Nova's life from her earliest memories until high school graduation. Her candid story chronicles many examples of how – with tenacity and the support of others – she faced and overcame adversity.

While working as a public school teacher and principal, I read aloud to students draft excerpts of Nova's autobiography; they listened intently, often sharing with their parents the poignancy of her struggles. The authentic enthusiasm of my students inspired me to help Nova edit and publish her story, which she hopes will build in those who read it greater sensitivity toward people with CP.

~ George Vernon William Kruse, Editor

AUTHOR'S NOTE

Why did I write this book about growing up with cerebral palsy (or CP as most people refer to it)? My purpose in writing it was threefold: to increase awareness about CP; to build greater sensitivity toward people with CP; and to inspire people with CP to lead more fulfilling lives.

CP is not a disease. However, CP is a *permanent condition* that occurs when a child's developing brain is damaged; it can occur to a child in the womb, during birth and up until about the age of three. In my case, the umbilical cord was compressed during a breech (feet first) birth, depriving my brain of oxygen and leading to brain damage.

CP can affect fine and gross motor control, ranging from light tremors to severe spasticity, from almost no sign of it to one being confined to a wheelchair. Still, it is important to note that *many people with CP have a normal range of intelligence.* In my case, it especially affects my ability to speak, use my hands and walk.

Few people understand CP. When able-bodied people encounter someone like me, misunderstanding is normal and avoidance is common; my slurred speech, spastic walking and shaky hands are unsettling for them. Often, people treat me as though I am mentally disabled or they simply ignore me. However, when people take a risk and open up to me, I am able to show that I am intelligent and, even more importantly, that I have a sense of humour. And by accepting and befriending me, they empower me.

Richard A. Watson wrote this poem about living with CP and the power of friendship:

A PRISONER OF DEPENDENCE

A prisoner of dependence am I
Whom fate convicted
In the delivery room;
Serving a life sentence
With no hope of parole.

Behind the bars of my handicap
I must make my life and career.
Through a crack in the wall
I peer upon the normal world
Which I can never touch.

Though I am serving time
For the crime of being born,
I am not shackled to the wall;
For I have friends who break the chains.
They set me free.

People with CP can – and should – lead full lives in spite of their condition. But they are too often told what they *can't* do, not what they *can* do. Caregivers can be over-protective and unwilling to allow their loved ones to take risks and try new things. My story demonstrates time and time again that the seemingly impossible *is possible* in spite of CP. My hope is to inspire people with CP and other disabilities to seek the support of others and, through determination, set themselves free.

~ Nova Bannatyne-Eng, Spring 2016

CHAPTER 1

споре этап

The first thing I remember about my childhood in Kimberley, British Columbia, is playing in the good old dirty mud puddles. And I remember playing sticks and stones, too – just like normal kids.

But right away I could tell I was different. For instance, I had to wear ugly, high army-like boots. I pleaded with my mother to buy me fancy new running shoes because my playmates would boast about theirs and then laugh at my 'funny boys' boots.'

Mom's reply was always the same: "Nova, Dr. Quille said those are the only kind of shoes you can wear, and that's *that*!"

споре этап

My family was closely knit. I can remember feeling like a queen sitting in my highchair across the kitchen table from my three older sisters, Nita, Jeannie and Florence. Mom would feed me, but if she was too busy or tired, my second oldest sister, Jeannie, would take over, even if she hadn't eaten.

Jeannie was always there when I needed her. She'd help me if I fell or if I wanted something I couldn't pick up. She even took me along when she went shopping or to the movies. And she'd always let me crawl into bed with her if I had a nightmare.

ᴏᴏ̃ᴇ ᴇ̃ᴏ̃

Early in the summer of 1960, when I was four years old, Nita, who was six, walked me to a nearby wading pool. I was scared of the water, so I just sat at the edge of the pool watching Nita and letting my feet get wet.

As we left the pool about a half hour later, we met up with some kids from another neighbourhood. They laughed as soon as they saw me and started to imitate the way I shuffled awkwardly along. I couldn't understand why they were imitating me, but I remember how awfully hurt I felt and how I cried.

Nita yelled, "Get out of here you stupid, dirty, skinny kids!" And then she ran after them and chased them away.

I was still crying when we got home, so Nita explained things to my parents and our two older sisters: "Some kids from across town laughed at her and they copied her way of walking."

"Why … the'-cop-y … me … Da'-dy?" I asked. "Why … it hur' … s'-much?"

Dad just stared solemnly at Mom and then turned away.

Jeannie, who was standing beside Florence, came over and took my hand. She tried to explain why I was different. "You're special, Nova. You have something called cerebral palsy … CP. Your brain was hurt when you were born. That's why you have to wear special boots and sometimes go to Children's Hospital."

But I was too young to fully understand and still felt hurt and angry.

ᴏᴏ̃ᴇ ᴇ̃ᴏ̃

Soon after this incident, Mom took me to Vancouver for what would become the first of many summer stays at Children's Hospital. I remember getting on a small propeller-driven plane with her and waving good-bye to my dad and three sisters.

We sat at the very front of the plane, but the stewardess asked Mom to move to the back because she was a heavy woman and there was too much weight in the front for take off.

Being left alone frightened me. "Ma-ma! ... Ma-ma! ... Ma-ma!" I screamed.

The stewardess, who was buckled in close by, tried to comfort me, but it was no use because all I wanted was my mother.

When we were air bound, Mom returned and held me tightly until we landed in Vancouver. My Uncle Bobby and Auntie Laura, my dad's brother and sister, met us at the airport.

I had fallen in love with my uncle during one of his many visits to Kimberley. He was the kindest person you could ever meet and full of fun. I hobbled excitedly to him, and he hoisted me up for a big kiss and hugged me like he meant it.

My aunt, who had a cigarette in her hand and smelled of liquor, kissed and hugged me too, but it felt cold.

After locating our luggage, my uncle drove us to his apartment.

I didn't know it then, but my Uncle Bobby was probably the one who was responsible for me learning how to walk. The doctors at home and in Vancouver had told my parents that I'd never walk. However, my uncle had proven them wrong.

Uncle Bobby would get me to hold on to a broomstick and then lead me around our kitchen with it. When I became steady enough on my feet, he'd pull the broomstick a short distance away and have me walk to it, challenging me each time to walk a wee bit further. In this way, little by little, I became better and better at walking by myself. If not for Uncle Bobby, I am sure I'd have ended up in a wheelchair.

During dinner at my uncle's apartment, Mom gave news from home in exchange for family gossip from the Vancouver area.

After dinner, my uncle tickled and teased me and then brought out a colouring book and crayons. I didn't realize it at the time, but I made an awful mess of the picture because of my CP; I couldn't coordinate my hand well enough to colour a pretty picture.

Still, I played with my uncle right up until bedtime while my aunt gossiped with Mom. Before bed we said good-bye to Auntie Laura; she had to catch a bus home to her apartment in New Westminster.

That night I slept close to Mom in the same bed.

∞⊙≥ ⑤⊙∞

When I woke up the next morning, Mom was busy making breakfast for my uncle and me.

I made my way over to my uncle's knee and he helped me to climb up. Then he helped me with my soft-boiled eggs and toast and juice. I don't know how Uncle Bobby managed it, but I remember that we both laughed all the way through breakfast.

After breakfast, Mom gave me a bath, and after dressing me, said, "When we get to the hospital, you be good. Do what the doctor tells you."

"Ca'-I-com' … hom'-then, Ma-ma?" I asked, but she just gave me a hug and told me to go find Uncle Bobby.

We left for the hospital with my uncle making jokes about

Mom's Dutch accent and her getting right back at him about his weight and bald head.

When we arrived at Children's Hospital, Uncle Bobby didn't get out of the car when we did – and this confused me. "I'd rather wait here," he mumbled, looking straight ahead.

Mom gave him a disappointed but understanding look, then turned me around before I could say a word, took me by the hand, and led the way to the hospital.

When we entered the huge lobby of Children's Hospital, I saw a few kids in wheelchairs and others on crutches. Mom pointed at something, and my eyes focused on a little rocking chair in one corner of the lobby. We made our way over to it, and in a commanding tone of voice she said, "You sit here and stay put while I tell them we're here."

Right away I noticed a gigantic teddy bear surrounded by children in another corner of the lobby. I wanted to go over and pat it, but I was afraid that if I was gone when Mom came back, she'd leave. So I sat and rocked.

When Mom returned, I pointed at the teddy bear.

"No, Nova," she said. "We have to wait right where we are until it's time to see Dr. Quille."

Instead of putting up a fuss, I rocked some more while she stood beside me reading a magazine.

Finally a receptionist appeared and said, "Mrs. Bannatyne, bring Nova this way, please."

Mom took me by the hand, and a nurse led us to a large room with four examining tables and then pointed to one in a corner. She drew some white drapes and it seemed as though we were in one small room. Mom began to undress me, even taking off my ugly boots. Then she helped me put on a little white gown.

Very soon Dr. Quille came in and greeted us with a smile. He shook my mother's hand and asked her if we'd had a good flight. Then he pulled a large red lollipop from the pocket of his white coat and said, "As soon as we're finished the examination, this is for you, Nova."

I felt afraid. I sensed the treat was his way of winning my trust, so I kept my eyes on Mom. As long as she was in sight, I knew everything would be alright.

First he took his stethoscope and listened to my heart. Then he stuck a wooden stick down my throat to check it. He also examined my eyes and did all the things my doctor at home did.

Next he asked me to lie flat on my back, and he put his left hand directly above me and told me to touch it with my right hand. I did that without too much difficulty. But when I tried to do the same thing with my left hand, it jerked as I raised it from my side. It took several tries, but I finally connected my left hand with his.

He then wrapped his cold hands around my right foot and pulled upwards. He did the same with my left foot. After that, he helped me up and off the table and had me try to walk along a white line painted on the floor. I did as I was told.

When Dr. Quille was finished, I immediately turned to Mom and grabbed her tightly around the neck, and she put her arms around me. He wrote on a note pad for a while before telling Mom that a nurse would take us upstairs. And then ... he left, forgetting about the lollipop. Mom and I stared at each other. She knew what I was thinking, so she reached into her purse, smiled oddly and handed me a box of Smarties.

Somehow I knew this was also an offering: it was a signal for her to return home and leave me in Vancouver.

"Don'-lea'-me … Ma-ma," I begged.

But she replied, "I have to go home, Nova, to look after Nita, Jeannie and Florence, to cook and clean for your dad."

Tears filled my eyes.

"Don't start that, Nova; before you know it, you'll be home."

But I wasn't the only one with tears. Mom was crying, too. She didn't like leaving me any more than I liked staying.

The nurse came in saying, "Nova, this way please," and as she tried to take my hand, I clung to my mother. There was no way I was letting go.

We entered an elevator and went up a few floors. As we exited we came upon a small boy wriggling and convulsing on the floor. It looked as though he had fallen down, so Mom reached down to help him. But the nurse said, "No, Mrs. Bannatyne. He has to learn to get up on his own without help."

"But he seems so helpless lying there. How can you watch such a thing, not pick him up, not show him some affection?" Mom had both sympathy and anger in her voice.

The nurse replied, "Believe me, it's hard, but that's what they're here for – to learn."

We walked slowly away from the struggling boy. I looked back as Mom dragged me along, and I noticed he was making a good effort to get up. But he disappeared from view as we turned a corner.

We finally arrived at a big desk where there were papers for Mom to sign. Then we headed to the ward where I was to live for the next two months. The nurse took us on to a big gate that separated the ward from the rest of the hospital. This is where I had to say good-bye to my mother.

She looked at me lovingly and knelt down.

"Mum-my, don'-lea'-me ... plea'-don'-go!" I cried, and I wrapped my arms around her neck so tightly that the nurse had to pry me away.

In the nurse's arms I kicked, punched, and screamed at the top of my lungs. But Mom, with tears in her eyes, turned and walked away at a fast pace.

The nurse let me down on the other side of the gate, and I immediately grabbed onto it and shrieked at Mom, pleading with her to come back. But she didn't look back; she kept on walking until she was out of sight. The nurse lifted me up and away from the gate and carried me kicking, screaming and crying down a hallway. She tried to comfort me, saying Mom would come back, but this made me kick and scream and cry even harder.

She took me to a huge room where there were about twenty-five beds, some with kids sitting on them. Other kids were playing here and there throughout the room. They all looked up as the nurse carried me to my bed. By this time I had settled down somewhat, but I was still whimpering and calling for my mom.

The nurse washed my face, took off the hospital gown, and helped me put on a little nightie that had been laid upon my bed. And then a second nurse appeared carrying my ugly black boots. When she approached to put them on, I began fighting harder than ever. Once again, I desperately wanted to escape.

I guess the nurses had enough because next they put me in a straight jacket and gave me a needle.

Soon I was fast asleep.

❦ ❦

In the next few days, I was a constant nuisance to the nurses. I would not stop screaming for my mom and other members of my family. As a result, I was moved to a smaller room where I wouldn't disturb anyone. But still I'd run to the window and wail hysterically. So they moved me from a bed into a crib and tied me down at night in a straight jacket.

       ✤ ✤

After a week and a half, I was somehow able to put aside the nagging need to escape. I began to cope better with the loneliness of being away from my family. I met and played with other children, and I went to therapy.

Each therapy session helped to develop my coordination and strength. Therapists had me walk in a straight line and match blocks that had identical shapes on them. Matching the blocks was difficult because my left hand was too shaky as I tried to connect shape to shape. However, lacing a big, blue boot that looked like it belonged to the Friendly Giant was pretty easy. And swimming, where a therapist took me in her arms and walked me in the water, was even easier.

One day, after many weeks without a visit from anyone in my family, Uncle Bobby visited unexpectedly. I was sitting on a chair in a corner of the hall and playing with a doll Mom had left when I heard the big gate open. As soon as I saw who it was, I threw down the doll and hobbled as speedily as I could to my uncle. He knelt down and picked me up, and I grabbed him around the neck and hugged him tightly so he couldn't get away.

The head nurse let my uncle take me outside where there was a swing, playhouse and sandbox. We spent the whole afternoon outside playing, and I remember laughing uncontrollably over one of his tricks. He'd ask me to twist his left ear and when I did his false teeth would pop out. I twisted and twisted that ear until it was so red and sore that he simply had to take me back into the hospital. It was the only way I'd leave him alone!

Uncle Bobby fed me dinner that evening. Unlike the head nurse who usually fed me so hurriedly that I hardly tasted the food, he took his time and pretended the spoon of food was a train going into a tunnel. Sometimes, though, he got me giggling so much I could barely eat.

Soon after dinner, visiting hours were over. It was time for my uncle to go. He promised that if I didn't cry, he'd come back soon. Then he gave me a tight hug and a big kiss, and he walked away without a look back – just like Mom did when she left me. However, I refused to cry because I was afraid that if I did he'd keep his word and not come back. I just watched him walk out through the big gate.

The rest of my days at Children's Hospital passed routinely that summer. After breakfast each morning a nurse would bathe me; then I'd play with some of the other children. I became good friends with a boy named Mike. Sometimes he'd feed me lunch, and before long the only time we were apart was when I had therapy. And of course another good friend was Uncle Bobby. He kept his promise and came to see me often.

⊷⊷ ⊷⊷

One day close to the end of summer, as I was playing with the giant teddy bear in the hospital lobby, I noticed that the hallway beyond was packed with people. I made my way closer to the crowd to investigate. As I gazed from person to person, I spied a familiar face. It was Jeannie!

As soon as I saw her, I took off, bumping my way through the crowd. It seemed that I ran a mile before my arms were around her, hugging her tight. And then I noticed that right behind Jeannie was Mom. "Mum-my!" I shrieked. She flashed a big grin and pulled me away from Jeannie – and she held me for a long, long time.

A little later, as a nurse led us to my room, I wouldn't move more than a foot away from Mom and Jeannie. It seemed like an eternity had past since I had watched Mom walk away from me at the start of the summer. Since she was back, I knew I'd be going home soon. I didn't cry as Mom and Jeannie left after visiting hours that day. Knowing I was going home had lifted my spirits beyond tears.

Two days later, Dr. Quille gave me the last examination of the summer with Mom, Jeannie and Uncle Bobby watching. "I'll be looking forward to seeing you next year, Nova," he said as we all left. Believe me, the feeling wasn't mutual.

We then made our way to my room where Mom emptied the contents of a brown paper bag onto the bed: a white summer dress, frilly white socks, and a cute pink purse with a shoulder strap. Jeannie got me all dolled up in my outfit while Mom went to sign me out.

A little later, Uncle Bobby was leading us through the big gate. I prayed I'd never see Children's Hospital again, but deep down I knew I'd be back.

⋘ ⋙

Mom, Jeannie and I spent two more days in Vancouver before we flew home. We stayed with Uncle Bobby, and on my first day of freedom he took us to the Pacific National Exhibition, better known as the P.N.E.

When we arrived at the P.N.E., everyone excitedly escorted

me to Playland, an amusement park. Jeannie took me on all the kiddies' rides, but unfortunately most of them scared me, especially the Ferris wheel, merry-go-round and Spook House.

On the Ferris wheel I cried and screamed for Mom because every time we came close to the ground I could see her but when I reached out for her we began to climb back up into the air. As we went up each time I shrieked and hung on to Jeannie for dear life. When we got off the Ferris wheel, Jeannie's arms were scratched raw; she looked like she had been attacked by some gigantic bug!

The merry-go-round wasn't quite so bad because I shut my eyes as it went around and up and down; and it helped too that Jeannie was right behind me. With her arms around me and her hands on mine, she helped me to grasp the pole and hang on.

The Spook House, however, was a different story. The halls were so narrow that I couldn't use my arms to help balance my spastic steps; as a result, I bounced uncontrollably from wall to wall and kept falling down. Jeannie ended up carrying me, but the eerie wailing coming out of the walls drove me berserk. I began to scream so terrifyingly she had to make a mad dash for the exit.

After the Spook House, I was so shaky and wobbly that I couldn't stand, even with help. Mom had to hold me in her arms for a long while and cuddle me.

Uncle Bobby felt sorry for me and bought me candy floss, but I made a mess of that, too. In no time it was stuck all over me, and my hands looked like they had little pink mothballs glued to them. By then Mom was exasperated, and trying not to touch me, she dragged me gently by the collar to the washroom to clean my candy floss coated face and hands. Mom and Uncle Bobby decided that the time had come to leave the P.N.E.

As we made our way to the exit, Jeannie won a teddy bear by playing ring toss and had a chance to try the giant slide. I made a few noises about going on the slide with my sister, but because of the Spook House there was no way Mom would let me. On the way out I thought about all the children I had seen – their smiles, their laughter. I decided then and there that the P.N.E. was strictly for normal kids.

ஒஒ ஒஒ

After breakfast the next morning at Uncle Bobby's, we were off in his car to the Vancouver airport to catch our plane home. My uncle told jokes and teased me right up until the moment he kissed me good-bye.

"I-lo'-you," I said in his ear.

"I love you, too … see you next summer," he said in mine, his words reminding me that I'd be returning in another year to Children's Hospital.

At least I'll see you again, I thought.

As we left Uncle Bobby, he was crying and so were we.

When we boarded the plane for home, Mom didn't have to move once she was settled because we were able to find three seats side by side at the back. Jeannie got the seat by the window, I was in the middle, and Mom was next to the aisle. After the Ferris wheel, I was nervous about being airborne again, so Mom and Jeannie each held one of my hands as we took off and kept assuring me there was nothing to be afraid of.

Once we had leveled out, Jeannie tried to keep me occupied by showing me how to use her yo-yo. I could make it go down but couldn't make it come back up; and I couldn't wind the string between the wooden spools to try it again because my hands wouldn't cooperate. After many unsuccessful attempts, I gave up, laid my head on my sister's lap and fell asleep.

When I woke up, we had already landed. My dad, Nita and Florence were at the doors waiting for us as we entered the little lobby of the airport terminal building. Dad lifted me into his arms and hugged and kissed me, continuing to hold me tightly as he gave Mom and Jeannie a kiss. After more kisses from Nita and Florence, we collected our suitcases and Dad carried me to the car, with everyone else following.

Florence, Nita, me and Jeannie.
All my sisters looked out for me, especially Jeannie.

CHAPTER 2

In my neighbourhood there were about twenty of us who stuck together, and I was the smallest of them all.

Whenever Nita and I headed off to a friend's house, she'd take me by the hand and lead the way. But when we'd arrive, she'd leave me waiting outside while she went in. I didn't understand why at the time, but it was because of my clumsiness and because I drooled so heavily that my shirt was always wet. Our friends' parents were convinced I'd knock something over or make a mess if I came in. I didn't mind waiting. It was a small price for what I got in return. I felt important being with Nita and the older kids.

Our neighbourhood gang was good to me. None of them ever teased me or treated me as though I was different. And when we went out of our neighbourhood and I was mocked, they'd stick up for me – and even fight for me if they had to.

Across the street lived another 'special' girl named Beth, but the kids in the neighbourhood would have nothing to do with her. They called her a 'retard.' Beth's parents weren't like other kids' parents; they were open and kind and welcomed me into their home. Whenever I visited Beth, we'd play for hours.

Even though Beth was five years older (about the same age as Jeannie), she liked playing with cars and dolls, making mud pies and pretending long sticks were horses – just like I did.

At the supper table one evening, Mom started talking to Dad about her: "I thank God Nova isn't like that. Remember the doctor who examined Nova a few days after she was born and said she'd be retarded? Then remember how Dr. Lang just laughed and said it wasn't true. If Nova *had* been retarded, I'm sure we'd have had no choice but to send her to a home."

Jeannie, who was feeding me, stared at Mom, horrified. Jeannie knew I had been listening.

"I-don'… wan-na-go … 'way … Mum-my!" I pleaded, and then I began crying hysterically. Mom realized what she had said, rushed over and picked me up. Her eyes were wide and apologetic. Dad came over, too, and he put his arms around us both.

Then Mom said, "We'll never let you go, Nova. But you will have to go back to Vancouver next summer."

I hated the thought of Children's Hospital but was comforted enough to begin to contain my tears. Before long Jeannie was feeding me again and my thoughts wandered back to Beth. I didn't understand what Mom had said about my friend. All I knew was that she was fun to play with. She'd help me cut my paper with her scissors, for example, whereas other friends and my family made me fend for myself, unless there was absolutely no way I could manage on my own. In my eyes, Beth was a good friend and that was all I cared about.

◦◦◦

In September, the neighbourhood children were off to school – everybody, it seemed, except me. Mom tried to explain that I couldn't go to school because I was only four, but I still thought it was unfair. Even Beth went to school. But Mom said that she went to a different type of school, much different from Nita, Jeannie and Florence's schools.

I didn't understand. All I knew was that every school day, once *Captain Kangaroo* was over on TV and Mom had begun to watch her soaps, I was bored. If it hadn't been for my dolls and stick horses, I'd have done nothing all morning.

After lunches and afternoon naps, Mom made me do therapy, and that never made me feel any better. It was as bad as spending afternoons back at Children's Hospital.

By four o'clock my sisters were home again. They'd take turns playing with me, and I'd ask about their day. I loved to hear about their teachers' antics and the games they played with classmates during recess and lunch breaks.

Not being in school, weekdays were long and lonely, but I didn't enjoy most weekends either. Dad was a heavy drinker, an alcoholic. On Saturdays and Sundays, even though everyone was home, we had to remain very quiet because usually he had been out drinking the night before and was in a bad mood.

Mom hated Dad's drinking. Almost every weekend they would have an argument for hours, until one of them stormed out. We'd sit quietly by watching *Sky King* or *Roy Rogers* or *Rin Tin Tin*. If Dad left, Mom would get us dressed and take us downtown. She'd treat us to a milkshake or take us shopping, I suppose to help us forget about Dad's drinking. Later, at home, if Dad hadn't returned, Mom would make us hot dogs or some other meal we liked. Then we'd settle down to some cartoons or maybe a movie.

Sometimes on a Sunday, whether Dad was hung over or not,

he'd make pancakes for the whole family. This was the only time he cooked. Mom would declare such a Sunday her day off, so Jeannie would be the one to feed me in my high chair. When Jeannie took a break or became distracted, I'd sometimes attempt to feed pancakes to myself, but this always ended in chaos. I'd get a couple of spoonfuls in my mouth, and then my hand would jerk spastically and pancake would just fly. Even worse, the cup of milk beside my dish would either end up in Jeannie's lap or on the floor.

Mom would get very angry and yell things like: "Why don't you just let Jeannie help you?"

I'd glance at her self-consciously, and she'd look away.

My sister meanwhile found these breakfast disasters humorous, even though she was usually the one who had to clean up.

Sundays often included getting dressed up and going for long drives. Sometimes we'd drive to the lake for a picnic, and I'd have a wonderful time playing on the beach with my sisters. My customary place was on Jeannie's shoulders. I was too slow and clumsy to race through the sand, so Jeannie's shoulders were definitely the best place to be. And anyways, at four years of age it seemed natural to be getting a ride on my big sister's shoulders.

⚬ఌ ౨⚬

I was also about four when I experienced my first Halloween. I remember that Flo, our name for Florence, dressed Nita up like a gypsy. Nita had cocoa all over her face, about eight necklaces around her neck, and the make-up was so thick around her eyes that she had trouble keeping them open. As for me, Mom wanted me to wear something roomy to walk in. She wanted me to be able to get up to doors with as little trouble as possible so that people could easily drop goodies into my bag.

Jeannie put cocoa on my face just like Nita's. Then she fitted me with one of my Dad's old hats, and I looked just like a rubbidub off the street. They even found an old coat that looked like it had belonged to a hobo. It hung down as far as my shins, but not so far that my big ugly boots couldn't add to the costume.

Once we were dressed up, Jeannie, Nita and I headed out into the neighbourhood. From door to door we went. Jeannie held my hand and yelled out: "Trick or treat!" and Nita and I watched our bags fill up with candy.

After about a half hour, I got carried away with all the Halloween excitement and tried to break away from Jeannie. But as I tried to hobble off on my own, I fell and skinned the palms of my hands and kneecaps. I began to cry so hard that Jeannie picked me up, comforted me and carried me home. Nita continued trick-or-treating without us.

Later, when Nita arrived home bragging about the extra candy she got, I was mad at myself for falling. I went to bed feeling frustrated and angry with Nita.

❧ ☙

One frosty fall day as everyone was heading off to school, Mom got me dressed to see Dr. Lang. I didn't mind going to see this doctor because, like Uncle Bobby, he was kind and full of fun. Also, unlike my visits with Dr. Quille, I knew I'd be returning home to my family.

During my visit, Doctor Lang used the same technique as Doctor Quille to check me over, but he talked gently and reassuringly as he squeezed my hands and the bottoms of my feet.

When he finished, I sat and played with his stethoscope while he and Mom chatted and went over a new therapy routine.

Later at home I attempted to walk lengths of our large kitchen, match wooden blocks to similar shapes on paper and lace up an oversized shoe which was similar to the big blue boot at Children's Hospital.

Also, I practiced eating by myself. I used a spoon with a large curved handle and a bowl with sections that made it easier to scoop out food. The easiest thing for me to manage at the time, though, was a two-handled, non-spill drinking cup. I could successfully drink from the hole in its top, seldom making a mess.

ৎৡ ৡৎ

Early in the new year of 1961, my sisters, neighbourhood friends and I played endlessly on the high-piled snowbanks lining our street.

In spite of the fun, I always ended up crying because I'd plant a foot too hard and unexpectedly sink like a rock. Luckily, Jeannie would come to my rescue, pull me out and attempt to revive my cold hands.

I hated the cold but loved the snow. It was fun making snowballs for snowball fights, even if I could never squeeze out a perfectly round one.

Ronnie, one of four boys who lived next door, would sometimes grab a hunk of snow and secretly make a perfect snowball for me. Then I'd stagger up to Nita and surprise her with a big snowball to the face. While she recovered and rallied her troops, Ronnie and I would giggle and ready ourselves for a replay.

ৎৡ ৡৎ

In the spring, when the soft snow melted away, I had to contend with concrete and pavement. Whenever I took off in an attempt to run down our driveway or street, my feet would become tangled up with each other and down I'd go with a cry of pain.

Since I was well known in the neighbourhood, there was always someone to pick me up, no matter where I fell. Usually, my palms and knees would be scraped and bleeding, so I'd be escorted home.

When I got home, Mom would always have the same expression: a look of love mixed with anger because I had ignored her warnings about running. After she had scolded me, she'd pass me to Jeannie who would clean away the blood and then bandage and comfort me.

When Mom had cooled off she'd sit me on her large lap and say: "Nova, you'd better get used to falling. Because of your CP, it'll happen a lot. Toughen up, and don't come home crying!"

In the month of April, there was a lot of excitement in our home because three of us had birthdays: Flo, Mom and me.

Unfortunately, Flo's birthday party that year didn't begin well for me. As the children were arriving at our kitchen door, two of Flo's classmates, boys from outside our neighbourhood, noticed me in my high chair. My hands were jerking as I tried to bite into a cookie, and they began to laugh.

Jeannie saw them snickering at me and confronted them, yelling: "Don't you know any better? She can't help it; she was born that way. If you pick on her again, you can leave!"

Even though my big sister had stuck up for me, I felt very hurt and hateful. I wished that, instead of scolding them, Jeannie had smashed their noses in.

The party to celebrate my fifth birthday went better, probably because only neighbourhood friends attended, our gang that hung around together. They accepted me the way I was.

Jeannie led us in all the games. In Pin the Tail on the Donkey, I won – but Jeannie helped a little. She said she was only holding my hands so I wouldn't knock down the other children's tails, but I knew better.

We also played Ring Around the Rosie, Little Sally Saucer, Hide the Button, and Catch the Ball. I ended up having a lot of fun because there was always somebody nearby to steady my hands so that I could win or come close to winning.

The party games were followed by hot dogs, Kool-aid, and cake with ice cream. Mom let me eat birthday cake and ice cream by myself. But what a mess! I had mushy crumbs from the top of my head to the bottoms of my feet and all around me – just like I had been dipped into a gigantic birthday cake.

ಲಿ ಲಿ

The summer of 1961 I returned to Children's Hospital, and once again I fought with the nurses, endured straight jackets and longed for my family. The last thing I expected was a miracle, but one came my way. The specialists who worked with me said the time had come for me to begin school.

When I returned to Kimberley, Dr. Lang agreed. Still, my parents were hesitant about me starting school because of my CP. Likewise, the school trustees on our local school board were hesitant; they decided that the only place for me was Pinewood, a one-room school for 'mentally retarded' children. At the time, that was okay with me. I didn't care where I went as long as I could be going to *school*.

Pinewood adjoined Kimberley's junior high school, but

regular students could only visit with special permission. My first day there was awfully frightening. We walked into what seemed an enormous room. At one end was an assortment of desks and a large circular table with chairs all around. Pictures were mounted here and there, some neatly coloured and some just scribbled on, like in my colouring book.

As we continued to survey the room, a grey-haired teacher approached and greeted us. She had a friendly smile and wore a red dress. It was then that I noticed children of various ages playing on a carpet at the other end of the room. A second teacher was supervising them. To my surprise one of the students was Beth, and when I saw her I relaxed a little.

The unfamiliar faces continued to scare me though, especially the older ones. Some students were older than Beth, and some were even older than Flo. And what a mixture! I didn't know the terms at the time, but there were deaf-mutes, children with Down Syndrome and a boy with cerebral palsy who wore hearing aids. There were also some children like Beth – almost adults, but very child-like.

The grey-haired teacher's name was Mrs. Atkins. The first thing she did was show Mom and me where I was to sit. Then, after a brief discussion with Mom, Mrs. Atkins informed us she needed to assist Miss Petrie, the other teacher.

Before I could communicate anything to Mom, she kneeled down, kissed me and said, "Now, do what you're told and you'll have fun. I'll see you after school." As Mom left and walked out the door, I felt deserted – like at Children's Hospital.

However, before I had a chance to work myself up into a fit, Mrs. Atkins was back. She placed a crayon in my hand and led me to the circular table where she had placed what seemed an enormous picture of a farmer and his dog. For a little while, she patiently encouraged me to colour the picture.

But I was more interested in watching others and observing their movements: Beth, her tongue hanging out of her mouth, sat quietly colouring; a deaf boy named Terry sat in his desk swaying back and forth, rubbing his hands together; four bulgy-eyed people about sixteen years old sat in a group at one end of the carpet staring absently at one another and around the room; another teenager (a girl who looked normal) sat at the other end of the carpet playing with a toy truck.

After a while, I got bored and tried to concentrate more fully on colouring the picture Mrs. Atkins had given me. Mrs. Atkins spent a lot of time that day pointing to words in colourful picture books. She also helped me try to connect pencil to paper so I could begin writing, but I had so much trouble coordinating my fingers to grip the pencil that my writing was mostly scribbling. Mrs. Atkins just patted my head and said, "It takes time, dear, but you'll catch on."

As time passed I became well acquainted with everyone. My relationships with the other kids at Pinewood were good because I was interested in and tried to understand their handicaps.

Terry, the boy with CP, wasn't shaky like me. He could colour inside the black lines of pictures, but he'd make the grass purple, trees pink and the sky green. And every time he finished a colour, down went his crayon and he'd rub his hands together.

I thought Reg, who was sixteen and had problems speaking, was pretty smart because he could give horsey rides. As he bounced me on his knee and tried to speak, I was in awe; spit would stick to his top and bottom lip, and I'd never seen anyone do that before. Reg and I grew very close. When our weekly gym class came around, he'd gently take my hand as we walked down the hall, just in case I fell. Sometimes Sharon, who was about the same age as Reg, would try holding my hand on the way to gym. But even though she seemed nice, she scared me because her voice sounded like a man's. So I stayed close to Reg.

Reg would also help me with my artwork. When I tried to dip a brush in paint, my shaking hands would cause the watery paint to leave the brush before I could get it to paper; but Reg would intervene and hold my hand with his, and together we'd compose a pretty picture.

Many of my other classmates were in their own little worlds. A girl named Cathy, who was big and fat, hugged a small teddy bear for most of the day. Phil was another student about Reg's age. He always seemed to be reading a book and taking notes. I'd have considered Phil just as smart as Reg, but his mouth was always rounded like a horse's. Also, when he got excited his hands would flail wildly, just like mine did when I tried to pick up or reach for an object.

My classmates who had been labeled 'retarded' became my good friends, and in my eyes the word began to have no meaning because these people played, cried and laughed just like I did. I considered them no different from Ronnie and the neighbourhood kids I played with.

Many adults didn't think the way I did. I had a neighbourhood friend named Theresa who refused to accompany me over to Beth's house. She said her mother wouldn't allow her to play with 'those kinds of kids.' She'd then tell me that I was lucky to be able to hang around with her. Theresa's parents tolerated me playing outside with her but wouldn't let me into their house. A few times I did ride in their car, but Theresa's mother would never talk to me. I quickly got the feeling that because I was different she didn't like me.

⊷ලෙ ෨ᨦ⊶

Going to school seemed to make time go by more quickly. Before I knew it, Halloween had come and gone, and Christmas was coming fast.

However, unlike me, many of the children in my class weren't excited about the coming of Santa Claus. It was as if they had never heard of him. A few of them did seem to have some understanding of the Christmas season, though. For example, my friend Beth wore a red coat with white trim on the hood that made her look like good old Saint Nick. And Phil said he hoped that Santa would bring him a gun on Christmas Day so he could shoot someone. I didn't like what Phil said; in fact, I hated anyone talking about death.

Even though Christmas wasn't fully understood by many of the children, Mrs. Atkins decided that we'd put on a Christmas play for our parents. The teachers made sure our parts were simple because most of the children had trouble concentrating. They explained to us that it would be a special play because we were special people. I could hardly wait to tell my family because they always talked excitedly whenever my sisters were in school plays.

We only needed a week to practice our Christmas play because the plot was very simple. And with much patience and coaxing from Mrs. Atkins and Miss Petrie, we were able to prepare a pretty good play.

Adorned with a crown and cape, I was Mary holding Jesus, a brand new baby doll. Beth was a winged angel carrying a wand

My class at Pinewood: Reg is on the left; I am seated centre left, dressed as Mother Mary; Mrs. Atkins is standing far right.

with a gold star at the end; she stood close by tapping me with her wand, as if to bless me. Terry, Phil and Reg were the three wise men; they walked up to me and placed gifts at my feet. Our remaining classmates surrounded us dressed as barnyard animals; they simply looked on and did as they had been told, which was to remain quiet.

Mom smiled proudly the evening of the performance, and our play was almost as good as Jeannie's, which we'd attended two weeks earlier. When it was over, everybody told me how much they liked it and how much they enjoyed seeing me as Mary.

Afterwards, there was a party in our classroom to celebrate a successful play and to usher in the Christmas vacation. But before we indulged in juice and cookies, the parents had an opportunity to take photos of us in our costumes. Mom had me sit on a desk behind some of the children so that my ugly black boots wouldn't show. She hated them as much as I did, and if there was any way to hide them, she found it.

Next, Mrs. Atkins announced that it was time for Santa. There was a delay for some reason, and then in Santa came all decked out in red and white, accompanied by Miss Petrie. It wasn't long before Santa was seated and my name was called out. "To Nova, from Reg," Miss Petrie announced as Santa handed her a gift.

I tottered excitedly to Santa who'd reclaimed the gift from Miss Petrie, and he lifted me onto his knee. At that moment I realized Santa wasn't Santa: he was Reg! I could tell by his hearing aide, and my suspicions were soon proven correct. When I reached for my present, my hand jerked and caught hold of Santa's beard, revealing Reg to everyone for a few seconds. Poor Reg! Luckily, few people seemed to notice, but Mom still gave me a dirty look when I returned to her.

After a brief but furious struggle to rip off the wrapping paper, I proudly displayed Reg's gift, a comb set for my dolls. Soon I was too busy with my gift to reveal anything more about Reg's new identity.

When my attention had returned to the party, Mom let me try to eat shortbread by myself, and this was somewhat successful. Juice, however, was another story; I crushed the paper cup Mom handed me and soaked my costume. My drooling of course added to the wetness, and I was soon so soaked that Mom abruptly wrapped me in her coat, apologized to Mrs. Atkins and Miss Petrie, led me to the door, and we headed for home.

॰ঌ৫ ৫ঌ॰

I have wonderful memories of Christmas vacation that year.

Sure, Dad had drunk too much on Christmas Eve, and he and Mom had fought, and I had been endlessly frustrated by one of my gifts, a dart gun into which I could seldom load the darts. Still, Christmas morning had been magical. My sisters woke me in what seemed the middle of the night, and we rushed to our beautifully decorated tree. At first I thought I hadn't received the doll carriage I'd hoped for. But after we had opened a few gifts each, Mom asked Jeannie to take me upstairs. My sister carried me to the closet that had big doors I could never get opened. Then she put me down and opened both doors at once, revealing a shiny blue baby buggy. I latched onto it and looked up at Jeannie.

She smiled, and I said, "Boy ... I knew ... San'a-woud-n't ... for-get!"

I carried my dolls and toys around in that buggy for the rest of the holidays.

New Year's Day, 1962, is also fresh in my memory, especially because I got to wear a brand new dress I had been given for Christmas. Nita had received the same dress, and we'd have looked like twins except that she had pretty socks and shoes while I had my big ugly boots with socks that fell to my ankles. But I didn't care, and everyone in my family told me I was just as pretty in my dress.

॰ঌ৫ ৫ঌ॰

Even though it had been a great vacation, I was overjoyed to return to school. We learned a new song the first day back. I loved it, and it went like this:

January, January, month of ice and snow,
January, January, soon the snow will go.

Mrs. Atkins played the piano, and all of us sat around her and sang. Actually, I just hummed because Mom had told me that it was better if I hummed instead of sang. She never said why, but I did as I was told.

Most of my classmates couldn't sing in tune, but they never seemed to care. It sounded funny when they sang, but they enjoyed accompanying Mrs. Atkins. Terry, the boy who was always rubbing his hands together, just sat and watched us. He couldn't sing or even hear, so I didn't blame him for rubbing his hands together. What else could he do? Sometimes we got to accompany with homemade percussion instruments. They were fun but whenever I tried to strike two of them together, I'd end up hitting myself. So instead, I mostly used my hands for clapping.

Winter was coming to a close when a class from the junior high school accompanied our special class to the ski hill for toboggan rides. We were to be well looked after: two junior high students for each of us. And as it turned out, two of Jeannie's best friends, Margaret and Yvonne, chose to chaperone me.

After arriving at the hill, the ski patrol led us to a small slope where we could enjoy our tobogganing. Since it was very difficult for me to hike up the slope, I sat on the long sled while my two escorts pulled me to the top. Then, with me snugly sandwiched, the three of us sped to the bottom of the slope, giggling all the way down. Our final runs of the day were the most fun of all because we challenged our fellow tobogganers to races.

Before heading back to school, we gathered in the ski lodge for some snacks and hot chocolate. Unfortunately, Margaret and Yvonne forgot that I needed help drinking liquids. They got me settled into a high chair, set a donut and Styrofoam cup full of hot chocolate in front of me, and then headed off to visit some friends. I was thirsty and the hot chocolate smelled delicious, so I made a shaky grab for the cup. In a few seconds, I was screaming because of the hotness spilling onto my hand. Even worse, my next reflex was to crush the cup, and this sent the rest of the hot liquid splashing all over me. I began to scream even louder, in pain and fear. Luckily, the hot chocolate had cooled a little before I grabbed it and I wasn't seriously burned; it was only hot enough to make my skin a little redder than it already was from the cold. Mrs. Atkins was the first to arrive on the scene; she rushed me to the bathroom to calm me down and clean me up.

୶ଡ଼ୡ ଡ଼ୡ୶

We participated in a number of activities with the same junior high class, usually in the huge gym inside the school. Under the direction of our teachers, these students involved us mostly in ball games and races. Because of my uncoordinated legs, I couldn't participate in the relay races. As soon as I tried to break into a run, my right leg would get tangled up with my left leg and down I'd go onto the hard slippery floor. So most of the time, Margaret or Yvonne would carry me.

Likewise, I had trouble throwing and catching a ball. Often, it was difficult for me just to hold on to a ball, let alone throw or catch one. And if I did manage to hang on long enough to toss one, it never went the way I wanted. So my partners, mostly

Margaret, would hold and guide my hands as I attempted to play catch with others.

One day while we were enjoying our gym class I saw the school principal talking to Mrs. Atkins and pointing in my direction. At the end of the day she put a note for my parents into my lunch box. "This is important, Nova," she said tenderly.

When I arrived home that day, the first thing I did was hand Mom the note. She explained, "It says that because the gym floors are slippery and your black boots scuff the floor, we must buy you some running shoes."

Actually, the note was great news to me. I was ecstatic because I had always wanted runners like other kids. There was one problem, though: I had been told that the only shoes I could wear were my ugly black boots. Mom phoned Dr. Lang to see what she should do. She knew it wouldn't be fair if I had to miss gym class.

When we went to see Dr. Lang, he checked my feet and legs and walked me back and forth in his office; then, as usual, he and Mom had a talk. As we left his office, Mom gave me the verdict. "Let's go buy you some running shoes!" she said, smiling broadly. I couldn't believe my luck. I was so thrilled that I pulled at Mom and tried to break into a run. But she began to get angry with me and told me to calm down.

In the shoe department of the Hudson Bay, I remember being mesmerized by all the runners. There were so many different kinds: white ones and red ones and blue ones, some with stripes or even Bugs Bunny on them. One kind even had the words 'left' and 'right' written on them in big letters so you would know which foot to put each one on. I stood and stared, deciding which ones I'd like. However, I noticed that Mom had gone over to the boys' section and was looking at some ugly black and white runners that almost looked as bad as my ugly black army boots.

"Nova, Dr. Lang said these are the only kind that will fit your feet and stay comfortable," she explained. "It's either these or nothing." Her voice was very loud, firm and cross, and people around us began to stare. I hated the thought of not attending gym class, so I had no choice. We ended up buying boys' runners without me even trying them on. Mom was too afraid I might cause a scene.

Even though I wasn't thrilled with our purchase, it didn't take long for me to feel excited once more. After all, I finally had my own pair of runners. However, my tiny bubble of joy soon popped. When we got home and I tried on my new runners, my sisters burst out laughing. They said they made me look like Bozo the Clown. I must have looked terribly hurt because Jeannie immediately apologized for laughing. She told me that the runners actually looked good on me, only they were a little big. "Nobody at school will laugh at your runners, Nova. They won't even notice," she assured me.

I believed Jeannie because one thing that the kids in my school didn't do was laugh at each other. When somebody did something funny or awkward, everybody laughed (including that person) or nobody did.

When I attended my next gym class, I wore those runners. Sure enough, not a soul laughed. I told myself that even if they were ugly, at least they were doing the job they were intended for, and that was the main thing.

Every weekday, I looked forward to heading off to school. And if there was nothing to do when the weekend arrived, I'd think of school. I'd think of how nice it would be to play once again with all of the so-called 'retarded kids' who were becoming my friends and a meaningful part of my world. I didn't realize it then, but I was learning just as much from my classmates as from Jeannie, Mom, and the rest of my family.

As my first year of school came to a close, everyone became excited about the places their parents were taking them during the summer holidays.

The upcoming summer was going to be an especially exciting one for my eldest sister, Flo. She was going on her own to visit my aunt and uncle in Manitoba. Of course I'd have to return to Children's Hospital in Vancouver, and that was certainly nothing to look forward to. I'd rather have gone anywhere than back to Children's Hospital. But no matter how many temper tantrums I had or how long I cried, I couldn't get out of it. I had to go.

Gently and sympathetically, Mom would try to explain it was for my own good, and that it would help me. But I still hated to go! Sometimes, I felt as though the real reason I was sent to Children's Hospital was because my mother and father didn't want me around; I felt they sent me to Vancouver to get rid of me. But Jeannie assured me they didn't like sending me there any more than I liked going.

CHAPTER 3

I made my next trip to Children's Hospital by Greyhound bus early in the summer of 1962. As usual, Mom took me and Dad stayed home with my sisters.

Even though I slept most of the way to Vancouver, I remember having a terrible earache going through the mountain passes of the Fraser Canyon. Mom encouraged me to swallow so that my ears would pop and relieve the pressure. But swallowing wasn't natural for me because of my CP; I could never remember to do it, which was why I drooled. Because swallowing was so troublesome, I got no relief from my earache. It was easier for me to fall asleep to escape the pain than to force myself to swallow, and that's what I remember doing. After an all-night ride, we arrived at the Vancouver bus depot with the sun beginning to rise. As our bus pulled into its parking bay, through the window I spotted Uncle Bobby, my favourite, waving and smiling on the passenger platform. Mom collected our luggage, but I couldn't wait. Like a pinball, I madly bumped my way off people and seats to the front of the bus, then hobbled down the exit steps toward my uncle. Before I could fall headlong out the open door of the bus, I was gathered into my uncle's arms, and I was kissing his neck and hugging him.

We stayed with Uncle Bobby all day and once more spent the night at his apartment. That night I again slept close to Mom. When she kissed me good night, she whispered, "Please don't be afraid and make a scene at the hospital tomorrow, Nova." Her words made me feel cold, so I snuggled closer to her and fell asleep.

After breakfast the next morning, my uncle bounced me on his knee, tickling and teasing me as usual. Then he said, "There are a lot of cousins I'd like you to meet, Nova. I'll bring them to visit you at the hospital." Again, the mention of going to the hospital gave me a chilly feeling inside.

Mostly, I kept my misgivings about another stay at Children's Hospital to myself, but on our way there I said to Mom, "You-gonna' … lea'-me-there … a-gain … aren't-you?"

"I have to, Nova. I have to get back to your Dad and sisters," she answered. It was the same old line.

⁊⁊ ⁊⁊

For the next week at Children's Hospital, I went through my customary crying and tantrums. But this time I was over the initial torment much sooner, and I warmed up more quickly to other children, their parents and some of the hospital staff.

My days included play sessions, therapy, the odd visit from a relative, and two hours of instructional time that was just like school. I guess because I had started school at home, I was given a chance to develop academic skills the teachers at Pinewood didn't teach; for example, I learned to count by threes, fours and fives instead of the usual ones and twos.

We did a lot of artwork, too. Unfortunately, I made a mess of the pictures and an even bigger mess of myself; it was the same as when I painted in Mrs. Atkins' class at home. Whether it was finger painting or trying to paint with a brush, my hands would jerk and paint would fly everywhere. Or just as bad, some other part of me would jerk and I'd knock a jar of paint over onto the floor. So even though I wore a painting smock, I always ended up being washed from head to toe after art activities.

Still, I loved finger painting. I especially loved dipping my fingers into the bright paints; they felt cool and gushy, like slimy snow.

Unlike Mrs. Atkins and Mrs. Petrie, at least the art teachers at Children's Hospital didn't try to convince me that colouring with crayons was my best talent so that they wouldn't have to clean up my mess. They even set aside my best paintings and sent them home to my family.

My coordination improved that summer. The physiotherapist explained to me that I was getting better at controlling my movements. I still couldn't handle small objects, and if I tried to walk too quickly my feet would still get tangled and down I'd go. But when I rode the special kind of trike the therapist had, my feet didn't get stuck in the spokes like they did in my trike at home.

I liked how the staff at Children's Hospital treated me just like any other kid. The only exception was that I had to wear a bib at mealtimes and one of the nurses or aides would feed me. I'd practice feeding myself in therapy, but otherwise I was fed.

Even though this stay at Children's Hospital was going better than previous visits, there were still occasional upsets.

I can recall one night when I became especially lonely for my mother and other members of my family. After crying for

Mom for a long while, I got out of bed, opened the door of my room, made sure there were no nurses around, and then hobbled toward the gate at the end of the hall. I was just about to make my escape when Mrs. Goodwin, the head nurse, emerged from a nearby room and caught sight of me. In a flash, she grabbed on to me and picked me up.

I screamed, "I-wan'-to … go-hom'!"

But Mrs. Goodwin didn't let go of me, even though I struggled furiously by kicking my feet and waving my hands. She called another nurse for help, and together they put me in a straight jacket and forced a pill down my throat. Back in my room, they stood over me as I lay in my bed shivering and whimpering for my mother, but soon I fell asleep.

Another time, I bit a nurse and a doctor as they tried to stop me from running toward the gate. And many other times, when the desire to see my family overwhelmed me, I threw books, crayons and toys.

❦❦ ❦❦

One special day, Uncle Bobby came to visit and brought along his girlfriend, Muriel, and her daughter, Monica. They entered my room with a basket of fruit and a vase filled with beautiful flowers. I was touched because nobody had ever presented me with such gifts. Monica was in her late teens or early twenties. She and her mother were just like my uncle, gentle and kind. If I tired and stumbled as one of them was taking me for a walk down the hall, I'd be delicately picked up and carried back to bed. Their words and actions were never rough or harsh.

Before they left, they took off my ugly boots and gave me a bubble bath. Besides being fun for me, the nurses loved it. I always soaked them more than myself when they tried to bathe me. This time, because I liked Muriel and Monica, I behaved myself.

After the bath, Muriel read me a story as I lay in bed. Monica tidied up the dresser and folded and put away my clothes. Soon I was falling asleep, feeling each of them kissing me on the cheek good-bye.

⋘ ⋙

Time passed slowly, like all my stays at Children's Hospital. Every second day Dr. Quille would visit my room to give me my usual check-up. He always had jelly beans or a lollipop with him. After putting a lot of cold tools on my body, exercising my muscles like they did in therapy and sometimes scolding me for drooling, he'd leave me with a treat and big wave good-bye.

Finally the day arrived when Dr. Quille informed me I'd be heading home soon. However, a couple of days later I was perplexed when Uncle Bobby arrived with Auntie Joey, my father's youngest sister. Mom hadn't come to escort me home. My uncle explained that he had decided to visit my family, and so he was going to drive me to Kimberley the next morning. That night, we'd be staying with Auntie Joey. I was very disappointed that Mom hadn't come, but I soon became excited about staying at my aunt's house. And of course my release from Children's Hospital also helped to ease my letdown.

As Uncle Bobby and Auntie Joey signed me out, I went from excited to ecstatic. In fact, the nurses told me that I had a bigger smile on my face than I had worn all summer. I said good-bye to them all, grabbed my uncle and aunt each by a hand, and practically dragged them out.

I had visited Auntie Joey's before with Mom, however we had never stayed overnight. My aunt's house was immaculate, like something you would see in a magazine. There were rugs from wall to wall, fancy furniture that always seemed to look brand new, pretty paintings, and everywhere you looked there were breakable treasures. There was even a different smell from our house, a smell so clean it was hard to believe that Auntie Joey's husband and two children also lived there.

When Mom and I had visited, she always kept me close to prevent me from breaking something or getting fingerprints on the walls. Mostly we had visited my aunt, uncle and cousins in their kitchen. That's exactly what Uncle Bobby and I did when we arrived there from Children's Hospital.

I don't remember much else of that visit, except that I slept on a wonderfully comfortable bed under a soft and puffy comforter.

Morning came very quickly, and before I knew it, Uncle Bobby and I were climbing into his car and waving good-bye to my aunt and her family.

My uncle's car was an English one, similar in size to a Volkswagen beetle. I sat in the passenger seat right next to him. Our journey to Kimberley led us through many mountain passes, where it was so hot that my uncle had to drive with the windows open. It was the kind of heat that makes your mouth parched.

Just like the bus trip to Vancouver, my ears began to hurt. Thinking that drinking something might relieve the building pressure in my ears and quench my thirst at the same time, I made a grab for an open can of Coke resting on the flat dashboard. But a hand spasm knocked it over instead.

"What are you trying to prove?" my uncle shouted.

It was the first time he'd ever yelled at me, but it wasn't

because I had spilled a can of Coke. I think Uncle Bobby was afraid that I could have just as easily hit the steering wheel and caused an accident.

My uncle's scolding hurt. Even though I slept on and off afterwards, it was more the ache in my *heart* than my aching ears that made for fitful sleep.

Late in the evening, Uncle Bobby and I arrived in Kimberley and soon were turning into our driveway. Jeannie was the first to come running out and greet me. Before long, the whole family – except for Dad – was out hugging and kissing me. Finally, Mom picked me up, held me closely in her arms, and with everyone else following, carried me into the house.

My Dad was nowhere in sight. When I asked Mom where he was, she responded, "Where else? His second home, the beer parlour." But she then quickly changed the subject by asking me all about my stay at Children's Hospital.

◌ᕙ᪥ ᪥ᕗ◌

In the few weeks that passed before school started, a lot seemed to happen to remind me how different I was from other children in Kimberley. At Children's Hospital, I felt as though I belonged. I belonged to a group of children with similar kinds of handicaps, but I belonged. In the real world, I didn't seem to belong.

As usual I spent a lot of time playing and hanging around with my sisters and our neighbourhood gang, especially Maxine Reed and my next door neighbour, Ronnie. The swimming pool was a frequent destination. We'd gather a crowd and head there full of excitement. Sometimes, in our rush to get there, I'd fall and skin my knees, but my adopted brother Ronnie would pick me up and carry me the rest of the way. Then, upon our arrival at the pool, one of the lifeguards would bandage me up.

The hot summer days just before school started always meant a huge crowd at the pool. I loved going there but was still afraid to go in the water by myself, especially because it was hard to keep an eye on the people I came with. Instead I'd wait on the pool deck until Maxine or Ronnie had their swim, and then one of them would carry me through the water.

One day, instead of waiting for someone to take me in, I wandered around the pool grounds looking for money or bottles to exchange at the corner store nearby. Near the changing room doors, I ambled through a cluster of kids who stared at me. One of them yelled out, "Hey, retard!"

I went a bit farther, managed to bend over and pick up a stone, and then threw it in their direction. That made the whole gang rush at me. Luckily, just then, a lifeguard came out of the boys' changing room. I recognized him as a high school student who had worked with our special class at Pinewood. His name was Joe. I latched onto him and stammered, "They … gon-na … beat-me-up."

"What's going on here?" he blared at the others.

"She threw a rock at us!" one of the older girls shouted.

"Nova, did you?" Joe asked.

"They-call … me-names; Mom-tol'-me … to hit … any-one … who-call … me-names."

"Why don't you wait on the pool deck, Nova?" And then he gave me a little push to send me on my way.

As I trudged toward the door of the girls' changing room, I looked back and some of the kids were mocking my movements as the rest laughed. Even Joe, standing among them, was laughing. This time, instead of feeling anger, I cried.

I managed to find my way through the girls' changing room to the pool deck, and it wasn't long before Ronnie noticed me wandering about in tears. He picked me up, hugged me, and asked, "What's the matter?"

As I explained what had happened, Ronnie tried to comfort me. He even told me that if he ever caught anyone teasing me again, he'd break one of their arms. This gave me an excited feeling inside and slowly my crying ceased.

However, there were many times when Ronnie or other friends or members of my family weren't around to protect me. For example, a few days later, as I roamed the pool grounds, I found a dime, enough to buy plenty of candy. I managed to pocket the dime and then made my way to the nearby corner store. However, I neglected to tell anyone where I had gone: I was too excited about my find and the candy to come!

As I arrived at the corner store and tried to go up the few steps leading to the door, my legs got tangled up and down I went. Since I was always falling, the first thing I did was look at my palms: no blood. Next, my knees: no blood. "Thank goodness," I thought, because my mother had a fit whenever I came home with anything bloody.

I struggled to my feet and entered the store, only to face a crowd of kids I had never seen before. They must have noticed my approach and fall because they were already pointing at me and snickering as I entered. My mother had actually told me to first ignore people who made fun of me, only hitting back physically as a last resort. This time I tried to pay no attention to my tormentors. I hobbled right past them and up to the counter.

I fumbled in my pocket for the dime, grasped it, and managed to drop it onto the counter. Then I asked the store clerk, "Co' … I-ha' … ten-cen'-wor' … bla'-juju' … plea'?"

The clerk, a pretty young woman in her twenties, must have remembered me coming in previously with my sisters. She smiled, proceeded to scoop a generous helping of black jujubes into a little brown paper bag, and handed it to me.

I grasped it as tightly as I could with my steadier right hand and then turned and headed for the door. Before I reached the door, I was confused because behind me I heard words similar to those I'd just spoken to the clerk. I stopped, turned around, and noticed that a fat, dark-haired boy had gone up to the clerk to repeat what I'd said. He purposely mumbled his words and flailed his arms, and all the kids with him laughed loudly at his impersonation. The clerk was laughing, too: I guess she couldn't help herself.

I felt like going up and kicking him in the shins, but I stared deep and angrily into his eyes instead. It was no use. The laughter continued and got even louder. I couldn't bear the ridicule any longer, so I attempted to hurl the whole bag of jujubes in his direction. As I did, the bag split open and my hoard of treasure scattered onto the floor, followed immediately by more laughter.

I don't remember much after that except that I didn't return to the pool and I was crying as I stumbled up our front steps. My mother was home, but she had little sympathy for me.

"You'd better get used to ignorant kids like that," she said. "Like I told you, Nova, ignore them. If that doesn't work, punch them if you have to. But whatever you do, don't cry. That'll please them, and make them tease you even more."

Jeannie was home, too. I remember her hugging and then tickling me to help me forget.

ༀ ༁

During the summer days that remained, there were other negative experiences with rude people of different ages. While my confidence suffered, nobody ever broke my will to fight back. If someone my own size and age was harassing me, one way or another I'd deal with the person myself. If the person was bigger or older, I'd memorize his or her face and disclose the incident to one of my sisters, neighbourhood allies, or parents.

As summer vacation ended, I made a vow: *never again was anybody going to get away with hurting my feelings.*

≈≈ ≈≈

CHAPTER 4

≈≈ ≈≈

B efore I knew it I was back at Pinewood for my second year with Mrs. Atkins and Miss Petrie. Little had changed since the end of June, and our special class quickly resumed its regular routines and activities. I noticed right away that there were a couple of new people. I also noticed that Reg was gone.

"Wher's-Reg?" I asked Mrs. Atkins.

"Gone, dear. He's moved to a different school," she explained.

This was disheartening because Reg had been my main helper. *Who will help me now?* I wondered.

When I told my parents my bad news, they assured me that other children could take over. But in my mind nobody could replace Reg.

That entire school year – grade one had I been in a regular school – I missed Reg every day. But I never saw him again.

Even though Reg was no longer a part of my school life, there was a primary supervising teacher named Mrs. Legget who visited Pinewood regularly, and she took a special interest in me. She was a tall lady who told funny jokes and made funny faces. Also, she could see right away that doing the same work as the year before was boring for me. So instead, she taught more challenging kinds of arithmetic: demonstrating how to solve simple equations with blocks, for example. Or she'd take me aside and read aloud from a book that would have been too difficult for any of my classmates to follow. Like Uncle Bobby, Mrs. Legget was genuinely interested in helping me overcome my disability.

Another thing she did was give me speech therapy for the first time. All I had to do was sit down face to face with her and repeat words like shout, shed, see, saw, look, like, and long. People always said it was difficult to understand my speech, which was odd because to my ears I sounded like everyone else. Mrs. Legget patiently encouraged me during our sessions and would even give praise though I wasn't pronouncing the words perfectly.

I also remember Mrs. Legget walking me up and down the hall for what seemed hours on end, helping me to walk a straight line. And when we had recess or lunch, she'd always sit nearby. She'd fill my cup a little at a time so I could drink by myself with less chance of spilling. If I had a severe spastic reaction and spilled my milk or juice, she'd quickly clean up and urge me to keep on trying.

But Mrs. Legget could be very firm with me, too. One day, as I hobbled home from school, two little boys ran right up on either side of me and mimicked my walk. I felt a wave of intense anger and I surprised them – and myself – when I managed on the first try to grab them each by the collar. "Take-th-is!" I screamed, and I bashed their heads together.

Even though the boys' mothers said "Good for you!" when I later had to explain my actions, Mrs. Legget wasn't at all amused. When I told her about the incident, she shook her head ominously. "Nova, that was the wrong way to show your anger. Never do it again. I'm very disappointed in you." That hurt me and Mrs. Legget knew it. Still, I respected her honesty and toughness.

Another time I got mad at a classmate for not sharing a trike. When he refused to give it to me, I kicked him in the legs and punched him in the head so hard his hearing aid fell out. Mrs. Legget witnessed the whole thing and immediately took me over her knee and paddled my behind until I cried. She then sent me to a little time-out closet where I sometimes went for naps, and I yelled and sobbed for what seemed like hours. When I settled down, Mrs. Legget made me apologize to the boy and told me I couldn't ride the trike for a week. I ended up with even harsher punishment than I'd have received at home, but Mrs. Legget had no patience for my temper.

࿐ ࿐

In September 1963, the start of my third year at Pinewood, a teacher's aide was hired. Her name was Mrs. Baglot, another no-nonsense woman who would not stand for any of my shenanigans. And even though we didn't get along very well at the start, she won my respect and I became very fond of her.

One incident I remember was when some high school bullies cornered a couple of my classmates and me against the fence at the far end of the schoolyard. All big boys, they pushed us down and then mocked our movements as we tried to get up. From out of nowhere, Mrs. Baglot arrived on the scene. She grabbed the biggest one firmly by the ear and thundered, "Just what are you boys trying to prove?!" She didn't stop there, but continued to scold them fiercely: "You ought to be ashamed for picking on kids smaller and less fortunate than yourselves! Apologize, right now!" Then she shouted, "Off you go!"

They went, too, and in a hurry.

From then on I saw Mrs. Baglot as a hero. She was a woman who was tough enough to scare off bullies and make them want to get away quickly!

She was strict with me, too, but in a way I didn't mind because she was always fair. When I did something wrong or got into trouble, she punished me; when I did something well, she praised me. Unlike many people who overdid praise, she just said "Good" or "Very well done" and left it at that. I always felt she was being sincere.

Mrs. Baglot left Pinewood just before Christmas break. While she had been there, I hadn't fought or fooled around nearly as much. Under her watchful eye, I had done my schoolwork, shared properly with my classmates, and cried out my frustrations instead of taking them out on others.

When she left, I missed her. But I remembered that she hated fighting and other kinds of nonsense, so I tried to behave.

During the Christmas holidays, I discovered that Mrs. Baglot lived on Sixth Avenue. We lived a few minutes away on Fifth. Sometimes, as I was playing alone or with friends outside, she'd drive by and honk.

Later on in the New Year when I had mustered up enough nerve, I trudged quite a few times through the snow over to her house. I talked to her if she was outside, but I never went in. Mom told me she had a husband and four children of her own and warned me not to bother her too much.

꧁ ꧂

One spring day Nita came home to say that Mrs. Baglot had just taken over the special needs class at her school. She explained that this class wasn't like ours at Pinewood. The kids had learning troubles or other disabilities, but they weren't like the kids at Pinewood: they wouldn't always be like small children, never progressing.

That's the class for me! I thought. I knew I could make good progress there if given a chance, especially if Mrs. Baglot was helping me.

Someone must have been looking out for me, probably Mrs. Baglot, because at the end of June 1964, Mrs. Atkins sat me down and said, "Nova, you won't be coming back to Pinewood in the fall. Do you remember Mrs. Baglot? Well, next year you'll be going to A.A. Watkins Elementary School, and she'll be your teacher."

I was speechless, and suddenly very confused. On the one hand, I was overjoyed at the thought of being with Mrs. Baglot and attending the same school as Nita. But on the other hand, I would be leaving the classmates I had become so close to during my three years at Pinewood, and I felt as though I was deserting them. All in all, I felt terrified by the prospect of such a big step.

Oh well, I thought, trying to be brave, *at least I have all summer in Children's Hospital to think about it.*

⚬⊚ ⊚⚬

My fifth summer of therapy at Children's Hospital was pretty much the same routine as always, with two exceptions. First of all, feeding myself was to become a regular part of my therapy. Second, I was moved to a new ward, a huge room with about 30 beds occupied by children of all ages who were temporarily sick, not permanently handicapped.

That summer, at eight years of age, I realized that it didn't matter where I was – in our home neighbourhood, at school, or even in Children's Hospital – there was always someone, big or small, who would mock me. Whether they focused on the way I walked or the way I talked or some other disability, it didn't matter: it always hurt. I kept my vow to stand up to the insensitivity of others; but as a result I got into more and more fights.

One evening soon after I arrived at Children's Hospital, I got into a big brawl with a boy in the bed next to me. It was suppertime, and he encouraged everyone to watch me struggle with the food on my tray. Pretty soon every kid in the ward was in stitches.

At mealtimes I did my best to eat among the others without making too much of a mess. This time, however, so many kids sharing a laugh at my expense racked my nerves; spasms made my arms flail and my hands shook worse than ever.

For a time I tried to proudly ignore the laughter, but then my troublemaking neighbour leaned over with a sneer and said, "It makes me sick to watch you eat."

The time had come to fight; I scooped a handful of steaming mashed potatoes and threw them into his face. He shrieked bloody murder, and the fight was on.

The brute was at least a foot taller than me, but I wasn't afraid. As he rolled off his bed over to mine, swinging his fist toward my stomach, my legs spasmed and I kicked him in the head. A second left heel to his temple triggered another dreadful scream, and very soon a nurse arrived on the scene.

"What's going on here!?" she screeched.

"I was just eating my dinner and she went crazy and started throwing food and kicking me," he whimpered.

"Tha'-a ... lie!" I cried.

But the rest of the kids in the room said it was me who was lying, that he hadn't done a thing. The nurse ended up believing the others, I guess because there were so many people saying the same thing and my attacker was in obvious pain.

As she took over feeding me, the nurse said, "Nova, as punishment for causing trouble, you cannot watch TV tonight. You can stay in bed."

Later on that evening, I cried in my hospital bed for my mother, something I hadn't done for a few years. It hurt so much to have been both tormented and not believed, and my anger, with nowhere to go, was almost unbearable. My mother would have been sympathetic; she'd have known I was telling the truth and the others were lying.

In the TV lounge nearby, I could hear my enemy and his allies chortling over some cartoon. Meanwhile, I cried softly in my bed.

ﾟoﾟ2ﾟ 9ﾟoﾟ

My stay at Children's Hospital went by slower than ever that summer, so when I finally returned to Kimberley, I was eager to enjoy the rest of the summer getting reacquainted with my family and friends. *After all*, I thought, *in one short week I'll be heading back to school: not Pinewood, but real school!*

Life at home, though, was no paradise. As I had lain night after night in Children's Hospital, I had recalled a more affectionate place. I wasn't home for long before I was reminded that there wasn't always love in our house.

If I dropped a glass of milk or had a spastic attack that sent my dinner dish flying or tripped and knocked a coffee table over, Mom still yelled at me. If she was in an exceptionally bad mood, she still swore at me or hit me. Even though therapy at Children's Hospital was improving my coordination, my parents never let me forget that I was still a challenge to look after.

Furthermore, Nita and I sometimes argued or scrapped over the smallest things; and Flo and Mom had the odd fight. And of course the Friday and Saturday night battles between Mom and Dad, once he arrived home from the Canadian Hotel bar, began again.

Thank goodness for tender, gentle Jeannie. If I became too upset, she was there for comfort. She could still hug all of me closely and rock me – so that I could fall asleep in her arms.

CHAPTER 5

The start of school was always exciting, but by the end of August 1964, I was beside myself with a mixture of nervousness and fear. My parents and sisters talked constantly about how things would be for me at elementary school. We chatted a lot about the people I would meet, and they reassured me that there was nothing to be afraid of.

Jeannie tried to describe Mrs. Baglot's ungraded special class. "Nova, it's not like Pinewood, but it's not like Nita's grade five class either. The kids in Mrs. Baglot's class are slower learners, but they aren't retarded." This was difficult for me to completely understand, but she told me that I'd soon know what she meant and went on to explain how lunch breaks would work: "You won't be separated from the other kids in the school. You'll have lunch with everyone!"

Mom warned that there would be kids who would tease me like the kids at the hospital, swimming pool and corner store did. "You'll have to try to ignore them, Nova. You won't be able to fight as much at this school." But she also said that I'd make new friends, ones that would want to stick up for me.

Pretty soon the big morning arrived, and Mom was getting me ready for my first day of elementary school.

Nita, who was ten years old, wanted to walk with her friends, so she skipped out the door ahead of us. Jeannie and Flo, both attending the high school where Pinewood was located, were in the middle of 'putting on their faces' but stopped long enough to see Mom and me to the door.

"Don't you look pretty!" said Flo before we left.

"Good luck," said Jeannie, giving my hand a squeeze. "I'm so proud of you."

When Mom and I arrived at A.A. Watkins, there were hundreds of kids milling about the playground that led to its entrance. Some were skipping or playing hopscotch, some were chatting in groups, and quite a few were staring at me.

Holding Mom's hand tightly and closely, I shuffled along with great concentration, fighting with every muscle to control my spastic steps.

Mom whispered, "Just keep your head up; don't pay attention to them." And we soldiered on up to the entrance.

As we passed through the front doors and entered the hallway, I noticed that every surface in the place was either freshly painted or spotlessly clean. Then a bell rang, and almost immediately a steady stream of kids began pushing past us. About five kids would pass for every step I took, and almost all of them glanced back. Some burst out laughing, but most just stared. Mom gave more than a few dirty looks as we made our way toward the office.

The principal must have been expecting us because he approached before we reached the office door, saying, "This way, Mrs. Bannatyne."

I was surprised when he led us down two long hallways to the back of the school and outside again. He then pointed to a dilapidated building with peeling yellow paint. It reminded me of the one-room schoolhouse I had seen at the Fort Steele pioneer village. "It's in there," was all he said, and he left.

A second bell rang as Mom and I reached the open door of Mrs. Baglot's classroom. Inside, I spotted about eighteen students seated in desks of various sizes. The class, like at Pinewood, was a mix of ages, from about seven to sixteen. At eight years old, it looked like I was going to be one of the youngest.

When Mom handed me over to Mrs. Baglot, all eyes turned upon us. The children seemed shocked by something, and I suppose it was my physical appearance and wobbly way of moving. They looked as though the creature from the Lost Lagoon had just walked into their room.

Paralyzing fear began to grow inside me, but before I became completely incapacitated, Mom said, "See you in an hour," and Mrs. Baglot led me to an empty little desk at the front of the classroom.

Mrs. Baglot got right down to business. First, she asked us all to stand and introduce ourselves.

When my turn came, I struggled up, and as clearly as I could uttered my first and last name: "No-va … Ban-na-tyne."

Because of my garbled speech, more than half the class started to laugh. Mrs. Baglot was going to have none of it. She pounded her fist onto her desk, took time to give every offender a stern look, and repeated my name loudly: "NOVA! … BANNATYNE!"

After that, no one was ever likely to forget it.

Next, Mrs. Baglot asked the class to copy a supplies list from the board. I didn't have a pencil and paper, and it was almost impossible for me to write anyway, so Mrs. Baglot copied the list for me. But when she handed me the list, I saw a familiar look in her eyes. It was the look she gave me at Pinewood when I goofed off or disturbed others.

"I did it for you this time, Nova. But from now on, you'll be doing as much of your own work as possible."

I could tell by her voice there was a slave driver in this person, and if I wasn't in line she'd soon put me there.

It was hard to get used to A.A. Watkins. There were so many faces I'd never seen. At recess and lunch, the children running this way and that way around the playgrounds made me dizzy.

For the first weeks, I played with Nita and our neighbourhood gang. However, my neighbour Ronnie and the other boys treated me differently; Ronnie spoke to me, but without a smile, and the others acted like they'd never seen me before.

In Pinewood I had been treated as an equal, and we had never mocked one another; but at this school, I soon became a target for steady ridicule. It seemed that whenever I tried to make my way from place to place, children would mimic my unsteadiness or call out: "Hey, retard!" or "Weirdo!" or "Slobber-puss!" I could never wander anywhere without being stared at.

Girls weren't as cruel to me, because Nita was often around. But the boys, especially the older ones, were relentless. Sometimes there would be a trail of them, mocking my every misstep.

I'd turn on them and shout, "Lea-me … a-lone!" But it was no use. They'd copy my words, making sure they twisted their mouths about and slurred their speech. I'd end up crying to Nita, and contrary to my mother's warnings, she'd encourage me to fight or throw rocks – and I did.

But no matter how many fists or stones I threw, there was always someone around the next corner of the schoolyard to remind me of my handicap.

.₀๑๏ ๑๏₀.

Fortunately, my lessons were interesting, and I liked how Mrs. Baglot made us take them seriously. She'd say: "If you don't want to learn, you might as well go live on the streets!" And if we didn't understand a lesson, she'd make us work on it until we did.

The biggest difference between my new class and Pinewood was that learning mattered. Mrs. Baglot insisted we do our best. She'd work hard to make a subject fun, and I loved how she'd tell humorous stories to spice up a lesson.

Because of Mrs. Baglot's personality and dedication, we all liked her and were willing to try hard to please.

My classmates and I soon became well acquainted, and as the school year got under way they came to understand my condition. Before long, if I had difficulties preparing for art lessons or putting on my winter coat, one of them was there to lend a hand.

The hardest thing to adapt to, though, was always being the last one finished. Because I had problems coordinating my pencil, the others finished their assignments much faster than I did. Further, my scribbled printing and attempts at handwriting were seldom readable. Still, by working one-on-one with Mrs. Baglot and speaking out my answers, I managed to keep up.

Near the end of September, I remember Mrs. Baglot announcing: "Next month I'd like to try teams."

What kind of teams? I wondered.

"It'll work like this," she went on. "The class will be divided into two teams. Whoever performs well in any subject will earn points for their team. At the end of October, I'll reward the team with the most points. Also, the highest scorer on each team will receive a prize. Every month we'll form new teams."

She then appointed two older students as captains, and they took turns picking their teams. It didn't take long before another girl and I were facing the rest, the last ones to be picked. I wasn't surprised when she was selected second last, and I joined the remaining team, the last one picked.

My team didn't seem very happy about having me on their side. After all, their impression was that I was slow at my lessons. Also, during P.E. [Physical Education class] games, I fell when I ran, or I threw the ball in the wrong direction.

Then and there I vowed that the next time teams were picked, I would not be the last one chosen. In fact, each side would be fighting to have me! Jeannie had always told me that I was just as good as anyone else, and this competition was my chance to prove it!

School became more interesting each day. I loved to learn, and my classmates soon suspected I was smarter than I appeared. And while nobody fought for me the next time teams were picked, at least I was spared the humiliation of being picked last.

Even though Mrs. Baglot's team idea and some of her other ideas were hard on us, she was sensitive to our learning needs, especially mine. If we undertook a class project, she always found an important role for me to play – like the time she appointed me as official 'picture finder' when we created a mural-like map of Canada. Because I couldn't draw recognizable pictures or even cut pictures out of magazines, I got to choose the best pictures for others to cut out.

I especially enjoyed it when Mrs. Baglot read aloud to us. When she read stories like *Treasure Island* or *Billy the Kid*, she brought the characters to life, just by changing her voice or the expressions on her face. Even though I liked to watch her read, I'd sometimes hang my head down, close my eyes, and imagine what was happening instead. However, when I did this, by the end of the story the top of my dress, blouse or shirt would be wet with drool. It was very uncomfortable to be wet, especially on a cold day. My mother didn't know what to do about my drooling. When I was younger I wore a bib, but I didn't want to do that anymore. So eventually I started bringing a change of clothes to school.

Inside my classroom, I felt pretty safe because our class was like one big family. Outside, however, a cruel world awaited me. As well as teasing about my appearance, children teased me about any peculiarity: changing my clothes during recess or lunch breaks, for example, or the way I ate.

I usually ate lunch with Nita. Mom told me to do this so that my sister could protect me, if necessary. Some of Nita's kinder friends would save seats in the lunchroom for us; but whenever she and I walked in, we'd hear groaning in every corner. Then when I'd start eating, many kids would look at me as though they were going to throw up, and they wouldn't stop staring.

Sometimes, I suppose for a laugh, a few kids would start imitating me: for example, jerking their hands up to their mouths. As soon as I saw this, my stomach no longer wanted food, and I'd push my lunch aside.

Nita would tell them off, yelling: "If it bothers you that much, don't look!"

The arrival of winter 1964, was also my introduction to skating. There was an outdoor ice rink on the school grounds, and Mrs. Baglot decided to take us skating during our P.E. periods. She asked everybody to bring skates. I assumed that included me.

There was only one problem: I didn't own skates. Furthermore, my parents weren't very cooperative. I tried to persuade my Dad to buy me a pair of pretty white figure skates, but he couldn't see things my way. He said, "If you have trouble walking, how do you expect to skate?"

When the day arrived for our class to head to the rink, I sadly said to Mrs. Baglot, "Sor-ry ... I-could-n't ... get-an-y."

She handed me a well-worn pair of boy's skates, smiled, and said, "Now that you have the materials, let's get you on the ice!" She then picked up a chair and led the way outside.

When we reached the rink, I sat down on the chair and two of my classmates helped me put on the skates, which had belonged to Mrs. Baglot's son. As soon as they were tied up, I tried to stand. Down I went. I then tried to get up on my own but could only flutter my stretched out legs. There was no way I could maneuver them behind me so that I could kneel and try to stand again.

It's no use, I thought, *I can't skate.*

Sure enough, every time my classmates helped me to my feet, I was on my behind in an instant, helpless as ever.

To put an end to my frustration, Mrs. Baglot decided to seat me in the classroom chair she had brought along – so that various volunteers could push me around the rink. But that made me even more frustrated! While the others were playing tag, broomball, hockey, or practicing figure skating, I had to sit on a chair and be pushed around like a baby.

Before leaving, Mrs. Baglot asked two of the strongest boys to hold me up so I could try shooting a puck with a hockey stick. I can remember standing supported between them, shaking and shivering like a dog, using the stick to steady myself. Still, I swung that stick so hard they had to duck. There was a loud smack as I made contact, the puck went zooming down the ice, and a mixture of shock and glee flowed into my bones.

My slap shot met with a loud: "Hooray!" I hadn't realized many of my classmates had been watching. After my experiences at the rink, I began seeking more and more attention from my classmates, and I became a bit of a class clown.

One day a doctor visited our class to speak about different health concerns: diet, exercise, skincare, things like that. Mrs. Baglot warned us to sit very still and listen. There was to be no whispering back and forth, no throwing things around the room, no cracking jokes.

When the doctor got to the part about avoiding acne, he went on and on, telling us what soaps to use, what creams not to use, and I quickly became bored. After all, at eight years of age acne wasn't a concern for me, so I grabbed my pencil and started scribbling on my desktop.

Unfortunately for me, Mrs. Baglot was circling the classroom and soon spotted me. She came over, snatched the pencil away, and placed my hands firmly upon my desk.

The doctor ended his lecture by saying, "Remember, boys and girls, an apple a day keeps the doctor away."

Before I could stop myself, I blurted back, "And-an ... on-ion-a-day ... keeps ... every-one ... a-way."

I guess I hadn't been the only one bored because the whole class broke into fits of laughter. Even Mrs. Baglot couldn't contain herself; she had to lean against some bookshelves because she was laughing so hard.

The doctor, who'd been stone-faced throughout his talk, never changed his expression. He just stood there dumbfounded.

Long after he left, Mrs. Baglot was still smiling.

✺

One day, just before Christmas holidays, a new problem began for me. Mrs. Baglot had shown us a film about leprosy, which portrayed the lives of a family of lepers. I felt sorry for them because, like CP, their disease handicapped them and seemed painful, irreversible and unfair. In the evening, when I was at home in bed, I fell into a deep dream about leprosy. I dreamed of a leper lying at the base of an erupting volcano. Streams of steaming lava were rushing down the slopes of the volcano, and the poor soul couldn't get up. As molten lava hit him, I awoke.

But somehow I wasn't completely conscious. Also, my mouth was shaking up and down in a crooked way and it wouldn't stop, and soon I could feel my whole body shaking.

I managed to roll off the bed onto the floor with a thump, but Nita, who was sleeping in the same bed, didn't wake up. Nor did Jeannie, who slept in her own bed on the far side of the room.

Even though I was shuddering violently, I rolled myself along the floor closer to Jeannie's bed, gasping: "Aw! ... Aw! ... Aw!"

Luckily, my gasps of desperation woke Jeannie. She seemed to understand what was happening because once she flicked on the light, she lifted me into her arms and yelled: "Mom, Dad! Quick!"

The next thing I knew, the entire family was looking down on me as I lay quaking in Jeannie's arms.

Dad then took me from Jeannie and told Mom to run a hot bath, and I remember returning to complete consciousness as Dad dipped me in the nearly scalding water and Mom splashed it on me.

My mother called this strange state a convulsion, and from then on I occasionally had convulsions, which woke me from sleep. When they happened the entire household seemed scared to death. I, on the other hand, learned to accept them as another part of my handicap.

CHAPTER 6

ᴥᴥ ᴥᴥ

A s the spring of 1965 turned to summer, my sisters and I got out of the house whenever we could. Jeannie and Flo spent most of their time with their boyfriends, and Nita and I usually went exploring with our school chums, Maxine Reed and her older sister, Lori. Whenever the four of us had money to spend, we'd head downtown for some excitement.

I can remember paying for many Saturday matinees at our local theatre. The movies were fun, but lining up wasn't. It seemed to take hours to get inside, and there was always some creep that insisted on making fun of me. When this happened, Nita or one of the Reeds would tell a story or joke to keep me from noticing.

Once we got in, I couldn't resist buying candy and popcorn, even if I always ended up getting more on the floor than in my mouth. I tried not to bother Nita, especially if the movie was a good one; still, if I found myself making too much of a mess, she'd take over and feed me.

Now and then, if I was allowed in, the four of us would wander through stores. One time at the Hudson Bay, Maxine persuaded me to take off with her so we could explore the toy department. It was fun looking, but it seemed that whenever I tried to play with a toy, I'd break or drop it. Maxine and I created a trail of destruction as we moved from aisle to aisle in search of something durable. Luckily, before we could attract the attention of some salesperson, our older sisters caught up with us and hurried us out of the store.

Another time at the Hudson Bay, Maxine and I broke away from our sisters and headed for the sporting goods department. We weren't there for long before we came upon a row of Mustang bicycles, all resting on double kickstands.

Maxine saw me eyeing a pretty red one like it was made of gold and said, "Nova, you're nine years old, and I think it's time you learned how to ride."

She then helped me get on and told me to pedal. I did, like mad, but of course it didn't go anywhere because of the stand. I was actually doing just fine, but then a spasm caused my left elbow to hit the handlebars of the bike beside me. Its front wheel twisted and it toppled into the one I was on, sending the entire row of bikes crashing to the ground, with me tangled amongst them.

The clanging and banging of bikes sent Maxine running, even though I was hopelessly trapped. She didn't want to be caught in the act.

I was too shocked to scream for help, but the commotion brought a couple of salesmen quickly to the scene. They extracted me from the jumble of Mustangs and one of them began leading me away, probably to see the store manager. Before we got very far, Maxine, Nita and Lori appeared.

Nita spoke up first: "Please sir, my sister has a little trouble with her body. She didn't mean to hurt anything."

The salesman scowled at Nita, but then seemed to understand.

He handed me to my sister, saying, "If you can't watch her more carefully, forget about coming in here again. Got it?"

"Yes, sir!" she replied, and Nita kept her word. She watched me like a hawk from then on.

I had many other rough and tumble adventures with Nita and the Reeds, many other times when I'd arrive home bruised or beaten up or exhausted. There was, however, one constant comfort: I could look forward to falling asleep in good old Jeannie's arms.

It was around this time, when I was nine years old, that changes in my family began. For one thing, my two eldest sisters were growing up quickly.

Flo decided to quit high school. She was spending most of her spare time with her longtime boyfriend, Stewart. He played the sax in a traveling band, but that wasn't the most impressive thing about him. He also drove a Dairy Queen ice cream truck! I can remember kids lined up at the corner of our street waiting for the truck to stop, but Stewart would zoom past them and right up our driveway. Then he'd jump out and talk to Flo while his partner served the crowd that had followed the truck into our yard. I liked this arrangement because even the jerks that made fun of me had to be nice if they wanted their treats.

Jeannie was sixteen, and something strange started to come over her. She had broken up with her steady boyfriend, and though she dated different boys on and off, she spent most of her time working at odd jobs. She seemed sad and would tell me things she wanted to do, like get away from home and live in a bigger city. Finally, she made up her mind that she'd be happier living in Calgary. My parents were dead set against the idea, but she was determined to go.

I remember sitting in her room talking about her predicament, telling her I didn't want her to go, either. "Plea'-don' … lea'-me … Jean-nie," I begged.

She tried many times to help me understand. But there was no way she could convince me that leaving Kimberley was for the best.

One night Jeannie packed her suitcases without anyone seeing her. She went to school as usual the next morning, but didn't come home. Later, she phoned us from Calgary. She said she was going to find a job and wouldn't be home until she felt ready.

I cried on and off for days after that phone call. Still, even though Jeannie stayed in Calgary for two and a half months, she wrote me faithfully every week. She even wrote to me in Vancouver as I later endured my annual summer stay at Children's Hospital.

⊶⊘ ⊘⊷

Three surprises awaited me when I returned from Children's Hospital that year. First of all, I was overjoyed to find that Jeannie was home for a visit. Second, Mom informed me that my doctors had given her the okay to discard my ankle-high boots. Third, she told me that we'd be shopping for my first pair of little girl's shoes right away because Flo was going to be married.

Even though Flo had been going steady for a long time, her marriage came as a bit of a shock to me. Still, it didn't take long for me to get into the wedding spirit, especially since it meant a new outfit and lots of excitement around the house.

My first wedding experience was an impressive one, because it seemed as though the whole city of Kimberley was there for Flo and Stewart. I sat through the ceremony watching the tears fall from my mother's eyes and felt very confused because I thought weddings were supposed to be happy events. My father, on the other hand, seemed very composed, and he sure looked proud of Flo as he gave her away to Stewart.

I wasn't as close to my eldest sister as Jeannie, but once I realized that she was leaving our family, I began to feel sad. As the ceremony ended, I started to cry. I remember running out of the church and begging her not to leave us. That started everybody crying, even Flo.

When the wedding banquet ended, Flo and Stewart drove off on a two-week honeymoon. Again, I was saddened. I wouldn't be seeing them for several months because after their honeymoon they were settling in Nelson, many miles from Kimberley.

As it turned out, there was at least one good thing about my sister's wedding. Soon after, my parents informed me that she was going to have a baby. So even though I had lost a sister, I'd be gaining a niece or nephew.

Better still, I also found out that Jeannie had decided not to return to Calgary. She was going to stay in Kimberley, continue her schooling, and work nights at the Grill Café.

঎ঌ ঌ঎

As I entered Mrs. Baglot's class on the first day of school that fall, I swelled with pride; my big ugly boots were long gone and I was wearing new shoes like everyone else. I can remember thinking, *At least there is one less thing to be teased about.*

Except for one new student, there were few changes to our classroom and class. We sat pretty much in the same desks as the previous year and Mrs. Baglot was as tough as ever. Right away she said, "I am not going to put up with any nonsense from troublemakers this year."

Later, she reminded me that I had been in a couple of fights the year before, and said, "Just because you're handicapped, Nova, don't expect to be treated differently from the others. You'll be getting the same punishment as everyone else."

I ended up testing Mrs. Baglot's warnings that very first day. I got into a fight with the new student, a boy about my own age who called me a baby because I was always slobbering. He wouldn't let up. He followed me around the playground during the lunch break, yelling "Baby! Baby!" in my ears.

When I couldn't take any more, I threw a rock and hit him in the head. He ran to our classroom crying, and I followed because I intended to tell Mrs. Baglot exactly what had happened. She hadn't returned from her lunch break, so we began arguing with and swearing at each other. Luckily for him, she arrived just before we broke into a full-scale fist fight.

Mrs. Baglot had each of us tell our side of the story. When we were finished, she turned first to the boy. "You should be ashamed of yourself! As punishment, you can be Nova's helper for a week." Then she turned to me, saying, "Nova, you could have done permanent damage with that rock! From now on, don't fight back, understand? See me, and I'll deal with anyone who teases you." As for my punishment, I had to help Mrs. Baglot tidy up after school for a week.

⚬⚬⚬

It wasn't long into the school year before Stewart phoned to inform us that Flo had just given birth to a baby boy, named Stewart Jr.

The first time I saw my nephew was also the first time I visited Flo and Stewart's apartment in Nelson. Mom, Dad, Nita, Jeannie and I drove there one Sunday. I remember pulling up in front of the apartment building, seeing a baby carriage resting on a ground level veranda, and Flo poking her head out of a nearby window, signaling us not to awaken the baby.

That day my father was all smiles because, after four girls, there was finally a boy in the family. He talked on and on about buying him baseball bats, balls and caps. Mom just sat there gazing at Stewart Jr. with love in her eyes. It sure was obvious that Grandpa and Grandma were going to dote on their first grandchild.

As we all crowded around Flo while she cradled the baby to comfort him, I noticed he had a lot of hair, light eyebrows, and big blue eyes like my Dad.

First Mom got to hold him for a while, because she was the proud Grandma who needed to burp him. Jeannie was next, because in a couple of months she'd be holding him at his christening. Then Dad, because he was the proud Grandpa who could sing softly as he rocked him. Then Nita, because she was going to be babysitting him a lot during the winter, spring and summer holidays.

Then it seemed to be my turn. My sister looked hesitant about me holding Stewart Jr. but Mom gave her a look that said it was only fair. As Flo put the baby in my arms, I almost froze where I stood. My right arm was steady, however I could feel my left arm starting to act up. Flo started to move away, but I shook my head to signal my sister to take her son back.

The rest of the day everyone seemed to give all their attention to Stewart Jr. Now that there was a *new* baby in the family,

even Jeannie got mad when I tried to sit on her knee. She wanted
only to dress, play with, and feed her sweet nephew. As I ate my
dinner, no matter how much trouble I had feeding myself, nobody seemed to notice or care enough to help me. So later, while
everyone else continued to adore the new baby, I sat outside on
the back steps.

Just after Stewart Jr. was born, one of our neighbours invited my mother to attend her church: The Church of Jesus
Christ of Latter Day Saints, the Mormon Church. Our neighbour
was Mom's best friend, and whatever she did my mother did.
Belonging to the Mormon Church meant you couldn't swear,
smoke, drink booze, or even drink tea or coffee. It didn't take
long before Mom was a strict Mormon like our neighbour.

I remember sitting in this church and watching my mother
get dunked in a small pool. After her 'baptism,' Mom started going to church regularly, and she enrolled Nita and me in Sunday
School. We learned how a fellow named Joseph Smith saw Jesus
Christ himself in a small bush somewhere in the United States.
Christ told Smith to write the *Book of Mormon*, which he did. It
didn't take long before I knew the whole story.

When the time approached for Nita and I to be baptized, two
'elders' from the church started visiting our home. One chubby
fellow took more of an interest in me. Since he seemed kind and
jolly, I chose him to dip me into the pool of water. I remember
fantasizing that I'd perhaps be healed of my CP when I was
baptized. But instead, after my chubby friend had dipped me in
the small pool, I came out wet and cold, and as shaky as ever.

Many people from all over Kimberley attended this church,
and they seemed curious about my physical condition. The older
members of the church were very understanding, however I did

get into a few fights with children who teased me. Since I always ended up being scolded for fighting in the Lord's house, I learned to control myself. After a while, like with any other place I had been in, people got used to me.

Jeannie joined a few months after I was baptized. I asked her how that would work because she had smoked since she was fourteen, but she told me she was going to quit.

At Jeannie's baptism, I stood up and 'testified' for the first time. "I … ac-cept … J e-sus-as-my … Sa-viour," I said at the front of the church. When I said this, I remember my sister and the whole congregation bursting into tears.

৽ৰ্ঞ ঙ্গৰ

Before I knew it another Christmas was coming fast. In Mrs. Baglot's class, we were working busily on a special gift for our parents. It was a wooden cutout of a rooster and hen to be decorated with different kinds of vegetable seeds.

When the time came to glue the seeds onto the wood, I had a hard time holding them. I could never handle tiny objects very well. Even when I managed to latch onto a few seeds, when I tried to dip them in the glue, it either spilled or I got too much on. I quickly became frustrated, because of course I couldn't glue on my seeds as neatly as my classmates.

It didn't take long for Mrs. Baglot to step in. She could see that I wanted my handmade gift to be as good or better than my classmates', so she ended up helping me finish it. On Christmas day, Mom opened my gift, a colourful, seed-studded rooster and his hen. "Nova, it's beautiful!" she cried, and I think she meant it. Right away, she placed my creation on the kitchen wall above the stove, and she raved about it all day.

Jeannie said she loved it, too. I remember her saying, "If you were still at Pinewood, you'd have given Mom and Dad another Christmas picture coloured with crayons. Way to go, Nova!"

Jeannie was good to the entire family that Christmas. She bought fancy gifts for each of us, but I considered my gift the best of all. It was a wonderful walking doll that wore red leotards, a lacy red dress and white shoes. It was the most beautiful toy I had ever seen. To show my sister how much I loved her and how much I appreciated her fine gift, I named my new doll Jeannie.

⁕⁂⁕

I returned to school after the Christmas holidays wanting more than ever to equal the performance of my classmates. But, it seemed that the harder I tried, the more frustrated I became. For one thing, putting pencil to paper continued to be a challenge. It seemed that the others took neat notes and drew proper pictures, while my notebooks were full of scribbles. Even worse, sometimes when I wrote with my big fat pencil, I'd slobber, causing the pencil point to go right through the paper.

I remember becoming jealous when Mrs. Baglot complimented the others on their good penmanship, an impossibility for me. Most of the time, she made me read my answers to her, but sometimes even I had trouble understanding them.

Thank goodness, my classmates often volunteered to help. The first ones to finish their own work would join me and act as scribes, writing down my answers. This made correcting my work easier for Mrs. Baglot and it made me feel better. My notebooks were just as neat as anyone else's!

In the middle of February, our town was filled with excitement because of the annual Snow Festival. The classes of all

Our whole class helped build a sculpture for the Snow Festival. My classmates had me make snowballs, but asked me not to squeeze them too hard so they wouldn't break. This alligator was one of the snow sculptures.

elementary schools were invited to compete in a snow sculpture contest. Our class was determined to win.

Mrs. Baglot led a class discussion on the topic, and we decided to build a lady figure skater with her right foot on the ice and her left foot a little off the ground. She'd be dressed as a queen.

Once the Snow Festival committee assigned Mrs. Baglot our location, we set to work. First, we needed three huge snowballs for the skater's body. I was an experienced snowman builder, so I had no trouble helping to roll up the snowballs. Next, once the three body pieces were stacked, it was time to shape the body with knives. But I didn't have a knife in my hand for more than five minutes before I cut myself. Unfortunately, that ended my career as a snow carver. I stayed out of the way for a while and watched our work of art take shape.

After a few days the sculpture was finished. My classmates

had transformed three balls of snow into a skating queen wearing a dress and a golden crown. There was some trouble getting her left foot to stay up, but they finally managed it.

When the Snow Festival committee later announced that Mrs. Baglot's class was the winner, Jeannie was even more excited than I was, so she rushed me over to take a picture. I didn't have the heart to tell her that I only helped make a few snowballs. Still, I made sure I smiled like a winner!

Like many annual events in Kimberley, the Snow Festival included a pageant at the high school to select a queen. A number of hopeful princesses would compete in a talent show to win the honour of becoming Queen of the Snow Festival. There were actually two talent shows, a matinee that elementary school students could attend for free and then the main show in the evening.

When I was in Pinewood, our class would be seated for the matinee at the front of the high school auditorium. Because I was attending a regular elementary school, I sat with Maxine, Nita, and Lori, deep amongst the crowd. It was a lot of fun because between contestants a rock and roll band played hits by Elvis and the Beatles. I just loved rock music. I liked it, too, when Nita played *Twinkle, Twinkle, Little Star* on her clarinet, but rock and roll was loud and exciting – and amongst everyone else I could inconspicuously bounce and bop up and down in my seat.

I remember the contestants coming on stage one by one to showcase their talents: one sang, one danced, one read a poem, and the others did much the same kinds of things, sometimes a little worse or better.

However, there was one girl among all the rest who stood out for me. She was very pretty and played the piano while she sang. Others had done the same, but there was something special about this girl. When I had arrived home after the show, I told Jeannie and Mom about how beautiful and wonderful she was, adding, "Boy-I ... sure ... hope-I'm ... tha'-pretty-when ... I ... grow-up."

This made Jeannie seem sad, but I couldn't understand why. I remember thinking, *Don't worry, Jeannie; she was pretty, but nobody is more beautiful than you.*

༺ ❧ ༻

Around this time, Jeannie's life changed. She began dating a fellow who owned a sports car. For a long time this new boyfriend never came into the house, but I'd always hear the rumble of his car as he picked her up or let her off.

One day as I played in our front yard he pulled into our driveway and parked next to a high bank of snow. I popped up from behind it as he got out of his car and nailed him with a snowball. He smiled at my surprise attack and returned fire. Soon we had a snowball war going.

I liked Gary from then on. Like Jeannie, he was kind-hearted and enjoyed playing games with me, reading to me or getting me down for a good tickle. Furthermore, he saw how Jeannie tried to teach me things like moulding plasticine or catching a ball, and often he'd join in.

Before long, Gary was accepted as one of the family. He even ate Sunday dinner with us and called my mother, "Mum."

༺ ❧ ༻

March arrived, and in Mrs. Baglot's class we needed to choose a project for St. Patrick's Day. She had plenty of art books, so we browsed through them, deciding what to make. In one of the books we found the perfect project, something we could easily make for our parents: a potato leprechaun. All we needed was a potato and some green and black paper for his hat, eyes, nose and pipe.

I wanted mine to be just like the one in the book, so Mrs. Baglot spent most of her time helping me. As we worked she asked, "Where do you want his belt? Should his hat be tipped a little or not? Do you want his pipe in his hand or mouth?" After pondering each question, I didn't feel guilty about her doing most of the work.

On the 17th of March we took our creations home. Mrs. Baglot gave me a lift so my leprechaun would arrive home in one piece.

Jeannie declared it was the cutest thing I'd ever made. She walked me up to her room and we put it on her desk. I sat on the bed admiring my work of art while she got ready to go out with Gary. They were taking Nita to Girl Guides and then driving on to Cranbrook to see a movie. Before they left, I threw a temper tantrum because I wanted to go, too.

"We don't mind taking Nova, Mom," Jeannie said.

"No, Jeannie. She'd be home too late," Mom replied.

This caused me to fuss more than ever, but it was no use. She had made a generous stack of sandwiches for the Guides, and I remember Nita, Gary and Jeannie each munching away on one as they waved good-bye.

Later that evening I got over being angry with my mother, and when I had my pajamas on she held me in her arms and rocked me to sleep. I was nearly ten years old, but I still loved to be rocked in my mother's arms.

CHAPTER 7

The morning of March 18th, 1966, I awoke to the usual sounds of my mother's heavy footsteps.

Why is there so much light coming through the window? I wondered. *Nita's up, but she didn't wake me. Am I late for school? But ... Mom would've called?* I got out of bed and hurried downstairs.

I found Mom and Nita sitting on the living room couch, and I could tell by their slightly bowed heads that something was wrong. I glanced at the mantle clock above our fireplace. It was after eight, the time we'd normally be heading out the door for school.

"You don't have to go to school today," Mom said in a very low voice. "Jeannie was in a car accident last night."

"Is-she ... hurt ... ve-ry-bad?" I asked.

"We're waiting for the doctor to call."

"Ga-ry-mus-ta-be' ... wi'-Jeannie? Was-he ... hurt ... too?"

For the first time my mother looked straight at me, and there was a faraway look in her eyes as the words came: "Gary's dead."

At that point my mind went completely blank for a few

seconds. Then I cried out: "If–Jeann-ie … is-in-the … hos-pital … she-must-be … all-right! Can't-we-go-to … see-her?"

No sooner had I asked that question than my Dad answered from the master bedroom, "Your mother and I spent the night at the hospital. It's best we stay put for now."

I sat down with Mom and Nita, and we began to cry. *Please, God, don't let Jeannie be hurt. Let her come home today, safe and without harm*, I prayed.

When Dad heard our crying, he called us into the bedroom. Nita and I lay down on the bed, one on either side of him, and he put his arms around us. My mother sat at the end of the bed. Except for our sobs, we were silent. We were all saying the same prayer – for Jeannie's safety.

Then the telephone rang, and my mother ran to the kitchen. She caught the phone on the third ring. "Yes" was all we heard her say at first. But then she broke into a loud scream: "Oh, my God! No!"

The next thing I heard was my Dad's fist hitting the bedroom wall. I watched as he pressed his forehead to his fist and leaned into the wall weeping.

Nita and I crumpled into one another, and I cried so hard my mind went blank again.

I slowly became conscious of two things: I could feel tears running down my face and I could hear Jeannie's voice. "Don't worry, Nova," she had reassured me once when I was little, "I promise I'll never die and leave you."

Perhaps it's a dream. I'll wake up any moment, I thought.

But no. My father, Nita and I made our way to the kitchen where my mother was still on the phone. "Thank you, doctor.

I know you did all you could," she said, tears streaming down her face.

Still weeping, my father went over and held my mother. Together they stood there, embracing one another.

⁂

Around noon, people from the Mormon Church began arriving with parcels and food. I remember the priest and others attempting to comfort my parents, who could not stop crying.

Members of our church kept coming. Some accompanied my mother to her bedroom and some sat at the kitchen table with my silent father. Others had Nita and I get dressed. They seemed to be taking charge of our house.

Later, Flo and Stewart arrived. Flo was crying as she stepped inside the house, but before Nita and I could approach, church elders surrounded her.

Nita and I eventually reached Flo, and together amongst many people we hardly knew, we cried for a long while.

What had happened to Jeannie didn't seem fair. Almost a week dragged by, and people continued to come in and out of our house as though we were having a celebration. Some visitors were aunts and uncles, including Uncle Bobby, as well as various cousins who had travelled to Kimberley for Jeannie's funeral.

The evening before the funeral there was an open coffin ceremony. Nita and I had never been to a funeral parlour before; when we arrived with our parents, we walked to the front past relatives and friends seated in church-like pews. We gathered around Jeannie's coffin, and I glanced nervously at my favourite sister lying there in a white suit. Her hair was nicely done and she looked as pretty as ever. She lay as though she was asleep and might wake up any second.

My mother took my hand and we began walking around Jeannie's casket, with tears rolling down our cheeks. I remember pausing for a moment as we moved closer. My mother pressed two fingers to her own lips then gently touched my sister's lips. But as she did this she broke down, and she had to move away from Jeannie's body.

I didn't back away. Rather, I reached into the casket and touched one cold hand. I said a short prayer to myself, asking God to look after my sister. But I was angry with God, too, because he had taken Jeannie away from me.

Later, outside the funeral parlour, everyone kept asking the same question: "Why Jeannie?"

ৡ৸ ৹৯

The next day our family rode to the funeral service in a limousine. Behind us was the hearse carrying Jeannie's body.

We parked at the front of the Mormon Church and made our way through a crowd of mourners gathered on the sidewalk. Standing alongside members of our church were many people I recognized: Jeannie's schoolmates, customers I'd seen at the Grill Café, and folks she'd say hello to when we walked the streets of Kimberley.

Seven men carried the coffin into the church. One of them was a former boyfriend who had once asked Jeannie to marry him. Even at a distance, I could see the tears in his eyes.

I remember the choir singing some hymns and the priest giving a sermon that tried to explain why God had called Jeannie. I also remember one of Jeannie's friends from the church singing a solo called *Beyond the Sunset*.

For the first time since I met him, I saw Stewart crying, like my father, and it choked me up. Still, I tried hard to hold back my tears. I knew if I started to cry, I'd never stop. Later, as we rode in the funeral procession and neared the cemetery, I noticed that cars were lined up for quite a distance along the route. In fact, so many people seemed to be attending Jeannie's burial that police were directing traffic.

The next thing I remember is standing in front of my sister's casket and looking back at row upon row of people lined up. They, too, were grieving the loss of a tenderhearted girl. Many of them knew how important Jeannie had been to me.

After the leader of our church said a few words and a prayer, the choir sang one more hymn so loudly that it echoed through the trees and rocks around us!

Before Jeannie's casket was lowered into the ground, six of her closest friends each placed a red rose on it. I finally burst out crying and wanted to run away.

My Uncle Bobby took me into his arms and held me tightly. "Shush, shush," he said. "It'll be all right."

After the funeral, many people returned with us to our home for a short rest before we congregated at the church for dinner. I sat in the living room listening to people talk about the ordeal.

One of my uncles came in with armloads of booze, and he and many of my relatives started drinking. The only one who didn't participate was Uncle Bobby (I'd never seen him take a drink for as long as I'd known him).

My Dad started drinking booze, too, like it was going out of style. This got my mother more upset than I had ever seen her before.

Suddenly she shouted, "You dare get drunk on the day that my baby is buried!" Then she picked up the beer bottle that was in front of my father and hit him over the head with it.

Our relations left the room, but my parents didn't start to argue as they normally did when Dad drank. Instead, they embraced.

I could see that my father understood my mother's agony, and for the rest of the day he didn't touch a drink.

⁂

A few days later, my father and I went into Jeannie's bedroom for the first time since the accident. I don't know why, but I felt a bit scared, maybe because I grew up thinking that death meant ghosts. Perhaps I was afraid that Jeannie's spirit would be haunting her room.

But the first thing I saw when I entered was the potato leprechaun I had given Jeannie the evening of the accident. At that moment it seemed an evil charm, not a special gift to her. Looking at it was too much for me, so I grabbed it, pulled off all the decorations and threw it out the bedroom window.

When my rage subsided, Dad took me in his arms and hugged me. Then we both started to cry, and we left the room. Neither of us went back for a long time.

The same day, my father informed us that he had quit drinking for good. Some elders came to discuss baptism with him, and he agreed to join the Mormon Church. From then on he came straight home from work and stayed out of the beer parlour.

⁂

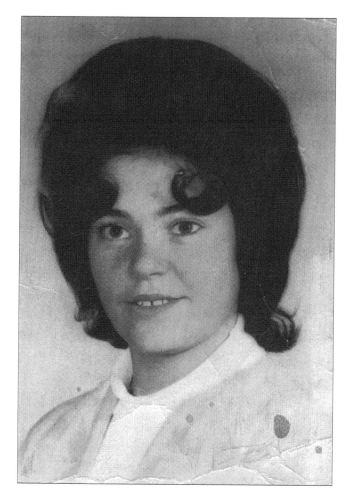

The saddest day of my childhood was when we got the phone call that Jeannie had died after a car accident.

Nita and I were away from school for almost two weeks, but it seemed longer. During that time, our family received scores of cards and flowers.

Mrs. Baglot and each of my classmates sent a card, so I made sure to thank them all when I returned to class.

For many days when I arrived home from school I'd read through the cards that had been sent to honour Jeannie. A lot of them were from her friends and those of my parents. The one that made me cry the most came from a family in Calgary. Jeannie had babysat for them. I felt guilty when I read their card because I remembered feeling jealous when Jeannie wrote about how good the children were and how much she loved them.

By the time April was well underway and my birthday was approaching, family life seemed settled again – except Jeannie wasn't with us.

The paper stopped writing about the accident, the man on the radio stopped mentioning it, and people seemed to leave it out of their conversations. I guess for our town the tragedy was over.

Our family's pain, however, stayed fresh for a long time. Jeannie was gone, but the memory of her lived on within the walls of our home. I knew it always would.

CHAPTER 8

ᕘᕚ ᕙᕗ

had my tenth birthday the spring my sister died. I didn't have much of a celebration, but that was okay because I didn't feel like celebrating. My parents said I was getting too old for a party anyways. Instead, they said I could have Maxine Reed over for dinner.

I remember opening my gifts after dinner. One of them was my very first wristwatch. Nita complained when she saw it. "I never got something that nice for my birthday," she whined.

I thought back to March 12th and recalled that Nita had received a necklace from Jeannie. I looked at her and said, "You-had ... some-one ... at-your-birth-day ... you-had ... Jean-nie."

Nita became silent. Mom looked my way as if to say I was right and then back to Nita.

"I'm sorry. I was being stupid," Nita said, and she meant it. That same spring of 1966 I had my first romance. It was love at first sight. When I returned to school after Jeannie's funeral, a few new kids had joined Mrs. Baglot's class. One of them was a boy my age with dark hair and baby blue eyes. When he walked into our classroom, I couldn't take my eyes off him. His name was Jackie.

Mrs. Baglot gave him a desk at the back of the room, not far from mine. Because he was new, Jackie was very shy. He hardly ever spoke, but sometimes he'd ask me a question. He also talked to a boy named Kenny.

Vicky, my best friend in Mrs. Baglot's class, would sometimes have me over to her house on Friday nights. Dad would drop me off on his way to hockey games and pick me up a few hours later.

One Friday night, Vicky's parents were out, so we looked up Jackie's phone number. After quite a while, we got up the nerve to phone him. Vicky handled the talking. First she told him how much she liked his friend Kenny. Then she disclosed that I liked him.

That phone call led to Jackie becoming my first boyfriend. Along with Vicky and Kenny, we'd sneak into a storeroom in the basement below our classroom to neck. Sometimes we'd even invite other members of our class, and they'd watch. Each couple had our own special place and we could spend the whole lunch break hugging and kissing. This quickly became the part of my school day that I most looked forward to.

⟡

Not too long after meeting Jackie, school changed again. One day before lunch Mrs. Baglot took me out into the hall. "Nova, how would you like to spend mornings with Mrs. Kerein and her grade three class?" she asked.

I didn't know what to say at first, because I was feeling very comfortable in Mrs. Baglot's class. My classmates knew me and understood my problems. They understood my funny speech and had long ago stopped teasing me about my shaky hands and wobbly way of walking. They could even read some of my handwriting.

Will Mrs. Kerein and her class be as helpful and kind? I wondered. *And will I be able to keep an eye on Jackie?* But in the end I told Mrs. Baglot that I'd give grade three a try.

Mrs. Baglot prepared me for my next challenge in her usual way by saying, "Mrs. Kerein is even stricter than me. You cannot afford to fool around and make people laugh. I want you to behave yourself, do the work the best you can, and make me proud."

As it turned out, my first morning in Mrs. Kerein's class was a lot like my first day in Mrs. Baglot's class. When I walked in, everybody looked at me like I was from another planet. I recognized most of them. Some of the girls I had played hopscotch with during lunch breaks. Some of the boys I had seen on Saturday afternoons when Maxine and I went downtown. And many others I hated because they had called me retarded or said I walked down the hallways like a drunken man.

Mrs. Kerein sat me near the front of the class, and it didn't take long before many of my new classmates were poking fun at me. In spite of hearing and sensing taunts behind me, I didn't turn around to confront anyone. Instead, as Mrs. Baglot had advised, I tried my best to do the work.

I remember that the class was learning to do long division. After Mrs. Kerein spent a long time with me explaining what to do, I got down to business and was actually able to finish the work. I felt proud of myself until we had to pass our papers to the person behind us for marking.

The boy I passed my work to took one look and said, "Mrs. Kerein, I can't read this."

"Do your best," she told him.

On that assignment I got eight out of twelve, even though only one answer was wrong. I went on to have similar problems in other subjects. My marker could never read my spastic way of writing well enough to correct the work accurately. Still, I made it through the morning fairly successfully. At least, at the end of the day, Mrs. Baglot couldn't say that I had let her down.

My parents were pleased that I was spending time in a regular class. They believed I'd learn even more from my new classmates. I didn't know what they meant at the time because I thought I was doing pretty well in Mrs. Baglot's class.

Mornings in Mrs. Kerein's class led to another change in my school life. My frustrations with printing and handwriting prompted Mrs. Baglot to think of a new way to make my work more readable. Because I couldn't use a pencil or pen well enough to represent what I had learned, she decided I should learn to type.

Actually, Mrs. Baglot was very frank. She told me that unless I could learn to use a typewriter, I'd never be able to manage in a regular class.

So what! I thought. I wasn't altogether keen to enter a regular classroom anyway. For one thing, I'd once again be leaving many close friends behind. And for another thing, I had convinced myself that I was in love with Jackie. Moving on also meant the possibility of transferring schools, and I feared that I'd gradually lose contact with my friends if that happened.

One day Mrs. Baglot approached me and said, "Nova, you should be able to enter grade four at A.A. Watkins next year. If you do well in Mrs. Kerein's class and improve your typing skills, you'll be on your way!" She was very excited for me.

Even though I loved Mrs. Baglot like a second mother, I decided to be deceitful with her. From that point on, I started purposely making mistakes, especially when I was in Mrs. Kerein's class. Even though learning to type on Mrs. Baglot's antique typewriter was difficult, I purposely jammed the keys.

Perhaps Mrs. Baglot knew what was going on; perhaps not. As it turned out, I didn't move on as planned. I stayed with Mrs. Baglot, Jackie and the rest of my friends for one more year, and again I spent mornings with the grade three class.

⊷⊙⊱ ⊶⊙⊱

Being with Mrs. Baglot for another year may have worked out for the best. It gave me much more time to prepare myself for the regular school system and to improve my typing skills.

As that final year with Mrs. Baglot progressed, I actually began to enjoy typing. I had already memorized the keyboard the year before, so it was just a matter of trying to coordinate and aim the less shaky index finger of my right hand. I never did learn to use more than that one finger, but I surprised myself at how good I got. I was still notorious for jamming the keys or hitting the wrong ones, but Mrs. Baglot's typewriter definitely made my schoolwork easier.

No longer did I have to wait for my classmates to finish their work so they could act as scribes for my assignments. I could do everything myself: Social Studies, Language Arts, Science, and even some Math. I still worked slowly, but I could work independently.

I also had more speech therapy that year. The lessons didn't improve my speech a lot though, because I never practiced. However, they did make me more conscious of my speech problems. The first time that the therapist taped and then played back my voice, I was shocked. Up until then I had thought I sounded reasonably clear, except every now and then when I bit my tongue. But after hearing that recording, I realized the difficulties others had in understanding me.

I was much more aware of my handicap as I approached the end of three years with Mrs. Baglot. Daily exposure to so called 'normal' children had increased my awareness. But, at eleven years of age, this made me feel even more self-conscious around my classmates.

Some children could only communicate by making fun of me, and some just assumed that I was retarded and therefore not acceptable in their world. But others were more sensitive; they'd step in when I struggled or include me in their learning activities so that I felt valued in spite of my CP. It was the strength these sensitive children gave me that helped me to finally embrace the inevitable.

At the end of June 1967, Mrs. Baglot informed my parents that I was ready for a regular class. All I needed, according to her, was a better typewriter; to keep up with the written work, my parents would need to buy me an electric typewriter to replace her antique.

CHAPTER 9

Throughout the summer of 1967 I underwent intensive therapy to prepare me for a regular grade four classroom. As usual, I spent most of the summer in Vancouver, but this time at two different (but related) facilities: Children's Hospital and the G.F. Strong Rehabilitation Centre. There was also to be a bittersweet surprise.

At Children's Hospital, my daily routines and exercises seemed more complicated than before. Still, I enjoyed most of my therapy sessions. I especially liked riding the exercise bike, using the boxing gloves and attending crafts classes.

After breakfast, my days always began with the exercise bike. I used to pretend I was riding down the Fifth Avenue hill back home. A mixture of friends and enemies would be riding ahead of me, and I'd pedal harder and harder until I had passed them all. Unfortunately, right about the time I really got going, the physiotherapist would tap me on the shoulder to remind me that I had done a mile and it was time to move on. Still, I sure loved speeding down that imaginary hill like a maniac, braving every curve all the way into downtown Kimberley.

With my adrenalin flowing, I'd head straight for the boxing

gloves. I always wanted to put both gloves on, but my therapist seldom let me. "You can only wear the left glove, Nova," she'd say. "Your left hand spasms much more than your right and will benefit most from this exercise."

But boxing was still fun because I pretended I was landing left hooks on some of the kids at school who made fun of me. There were a couple of them I sure messed up!

My fondest memories of crafts classes were of a helper named Mrs. Braiden and a leather wallet project.

I was very impressed with Mrs. Braiden because she wasn't much taller than I was. I had only seen people like her in the circus. She was what some people call a 'midget.' As time went by, we became very close because she'd kid around with me and I'd give it right back to her.

One day Mrs. Braiden discovered a wallet pattern in a magazine, a simple design, and she showed it to me. "If I cut out the leather pieces, I think you can do the rest," she said. "It'll have a compartment for change, one for bills and papers and a clear plastic one for I.D."

Using a hole punch and a needle strung with cord, I slowly pieced the leather together with only a little help from Mrs. Braiden; and even though I poked myself many times with the needle, I didn't give up until I'd finished.

Because that wallet was the first craft I had completed almost entirely on my own, I'd proudly show it off to Uncle Bobby or anyone else who visited.

Therapy at G.F. Strong was a pleasant break from Children's Hospital. And as long as a family member joined me, I was able to stay nearby at Easter Seal House.

I remember being thrilled when Mom was able to make the

trip from Kimberley. We had our own little apartment with two bedrooms, a living room, bathroom and kitchen. Each morning some man in a station wagon would pick us up and take us to the centre. These special arrangements made my daily sessions at G.F. Strong something to look forward to.

I underwent therapy there for a couple of weeks. In addition to trying out various styles of electric typewriters and new twists to my regular exercises, I had speech therapy.

With her teeth at my eye level, the therapist would exaggerate a 'sh' or a 'ch' or some other sound and have me watch carefully. She'd then show me where to put my tongue to make the correct sounds.

I bit my tongue more than a few times as I practiced, and my jaw would ache at the end of each session. I couldn't really sense any difference in my speech, but my mother assured me that the intensive therapy was helping.

It was around the time of my stay at G.F. Strong that I became a test case for an important surgical procedure.

A Vancouver specialist named Dr. Wilkie had developed a way of controlling saliva in cases like mine. The procedure had never been performed on a human being, but experiments had shown it could be done.

I knew that everyone in my family hated my drooling problem as much as I did. My mother often complained about the fronts of my dresses and coats always being wet, and constantly changing my clothing meant lots of extra laundry for her.

Since my slobbering was as bad as ever and I was getting too old for bibs, she felt the operation was worth a try. So before my Mom returned to Kimberley, she gave her permission for the operation to be done as soon as possible.

I was terrified about being operated on, but there was one ray of hope. Before my mother left, Dr. Wilkie said, "Because there are some serious risks, Mrs. Bannatyne, we won't operate if Nova's drooling by chance improves in the next little while."

Naturally, after hearing that, I did my best to stop drooling when I returned to Children's Hospital. For a while I did a pretty good job of controlling my saliva; for the first time in my life I was able to wear the same dress all day. I remember the nurses being very impressed. The way they talked, I thought for sure I'd escape the operation.

The only one who wasn't convinced was Dr. Wilkie. He looked skeptical every time he visited. I think he suspected I was wiping my saliva away with a Kleenex.

About three weeks before I was to return to Kimberley, Dr. Wilkie came to tell me that the operation would be going ahead, the very next day. "To prepare your system for the operation, you won't be able to eat breakfast tomorrow morning. You can drink a little water this evening, but that's all," he said.

Sometime before noon the next day a nurse gave me a needle in my bottom. I don't remember seeing Dr. Wilkie before my operation, and I lost consciousness as I was being wheeled into an operating room in another section of Children's Hospital.

When I awoke from the operation, I sensed I was back on my own ward. However, it seemed I had been placed in one of the smaller, private rooms used for very sick children. It was dark, and I was alone.

A little while after I got my bearings, I felt my left cheek. It seemed immense! Thinking that they had made me into some kind of monster, I began to cry.

I was awake and sobbing quite a few minutes. No nurses

appeared, so I decided to take a look at my face. I got out of bed, opened the door, and very quietly headed for the washroom. I entered and rushed to the mirror. My left cheek was so swollen that my left eye was closed tight. Seeing this, I let out a big yell, which brought a nurse running into the room.

The nurse calmed me down and then escorted me back to bed, where she gave me a needle. She spent a little more time comforting me, assuring me that my face would be back to normal in a couple of days.

But soon I didn't care: I was out cold.

The next morning, I woke up around nine o'clock. The sun was shining brightly through the curtains of my room. I called for a nurse and one came within seconds. I had to go to the bathroom, but she told me to use the bedpan. I wasn't allowed out of bed.

When she left my room with the bedpan, I slid down to the table at the end of the bed. The middle opened up, revealing a mirror, so I took a look at my face. The swelling had come down a little. My eye was open, but my cheek still looked like there were a dozen marbles stuffed into it. I couldn't help letting out a little whine, which brought the nurse running again.

"Your face won't stay like that forever," she assured me. She then gave me a sponge bath to calm me down and later brought a vanilla milkshake, which I drank through a straw. I could barely open my mouth.

By the time Dr. Wilkie came in to see what a good job he had done, I was getting used to the mess my face was in. Just like the nurses, he told me not to worry. "Your face is supposed to be swollen," he said. "If it wasn't, it would be a sign that your operation was unsuccessful. But Nova, the job is only half done. I still have to operate on the right side."

Before he left, he gave me two baby teeth he had removed and said, "I also had to remove your adenoids and tonsils – four operations in one! Next time it won't be so bad."

In about three days my cheek was back to normal, and I was back in a larger room with other children. I was eating regular meals again and a little bit between meals, too. Even better, I had no pain. It wasn't long, though, before I was being told that my second operation would happen any day.

In the meantime, I got some very good news. A nurse named Mrs. MacDonald read to me a letter from my Dad. Flo now had a second baby, another boy. Dad had been sending letters all summer, which was a first for him. I guess since he wasn't drinking and not spending most of his free time in pubs, he had the time to write.

The day after receiving Dad's letter, I was surprised to hear my parents in the hall outside my room. "Can-we … pleas' … go-home?" I begged when they entered.

"No," they said, because they knew about the second operation.

"Don't worry, Nova," said Mom. "We're going to be staying here in Vancouver until you are ready to leave the hospital."

"That's right. I've taken two weeks holidays, so we'll be able to visit you every day until it's time to go," said Dad.

"Where-'s … Ni-ta?" I asked.

They explained that she was in Nelson helping Flo out. We'd be picking her up on our way back to Kimberley.

The night before my final operation, my parents visited. After sitting and playing with me, they left giving me their word that they would be there the next day when I came to.

After my parents left, Mrs. MacDonald came in to remind me that I could have nothing to eat or drink in the morning. She also reassured me that my cheek wouldn't react as severely this time. Still, I hardly slept.

I had barely woken up the next morning before I was given a needle. As I fell unconscious, I prayed I'd never again have to endure another operation.

Later that night, I awoke in a slightly larger private room. My parents were nowhere in sight. I was alone. I felt the right side of my face; it was swollen, but I didn't know how badly. I wanted to see it. However, this time I was tied down in my bed so I couldn't get up. I was still weak from the operation, so I let myself fall asleep.

When I woke up the next morning, a nurse was there with my bedpan. I still wasn't allowed to get out of bed, but someone had placed a mirror within reach, so I held it up to my face. Dr. Wilkie hadn't lied to me; my face wasn't as bad as before. It still looked like I had marbles in my mouth, but only a few.

I asked the nurse where my parents were. She said they had phoned, but wouldn't be coming until 2:00 o'clock that afternoon, when visiting hours began.

Around noon, Dr. Wilkie dropped by. He'd just come from surgery, so he was wearing his green operating gown. He felt my face, pressing hard in some places and lightly in others. As he did, he asked where it hurt. Everywhere he touched was painful.

"You have stitches in your mouth, so you need to be careful for a few days," he said. "But I won't have to take them out. They'll dissolve on their own."

About an hour after Dr. Wilkie left, my parents finally arrived to see me. They sat down on either side of my bed, and Mom said, "My God, Nova, your face looks horrible."

If only she had seen it the first time! I thought.

Before they left, Dad shared some good news. "I've spoken to Dr. Wilkie and it looks like both operations were a success. If there are no complications, you'll be able to leave as soon as the swelling comes down."

Four days later, I was released and on my way. My parents drove non-stop to Nelson so I could see my new nephew.

CHAPTER 10

ஒஓ ஓஓ

All the way to Nelson, I considered the hurdles awaiting me in the fall when I would enter grade four. I'd be in a regular class all day for the first time. Somehow I'd have to cope with being the only handicapped person in a class of so-called 'normal kids.' Everyone was pulling for me to make a success of it, and I knew I'd have to put in my biggest effort ever to live up to their hopes for me.

Mrs. Baglot had worked hard to get me into a regular class, but she was a little worried about how I'd behave. I thought back to one day late in June when she sat me down and warned that I'd have to change my ways: "You'll be in a class of over thirty students. You won't be allowed to distract people the way you do in my class. No talking out loud and playing tricks to get attention. All that will have to stop."

Mrs. Baglot had been very firm with me that day, but I didn't mind her advice. She had helped me in so many ways and was proud of me. I knew I'd miss my 'second mother' very much.

My parents were also proud, but they, too, had warnings. "Be prepared for more name calling and teasing," my mother cautioned. "Don't forget that you're two years older than most of the children. Some of them will have trouble understanding your handicap, especially at the start."

I remember my father saying, "Because of your CP, you'll have to work much harder than the other kids, just to keep up."

"Keeping up," however, would be more manageable with the new electric typewriter my dad had ordered before we left Vancouver. The therapists at G.F. Strong had recommended a modified model that seemed to best suit my needs. It was going to be a lot different from the antique model I had used in Mrs. Baglot's class. I especially liked one special feature: a flexible plastic skin covered the keys to prevent me from making so many mistakes.

As we made our way to Flo's, I tried to think positively about my move to a regular classroom. I was still facing obstacles, but at least I had overcome two of them: I'd no longer be drooling and I'd be able to write more easily.

⊙❧ ❧⊙

I began the school year with a fashionable haircut for 1967. Our neighbour, a hairdresser in training, gave me a 'pixie cut,' which looked terrific, and I got a lot of compliments. It was practical, too. Because my hair was short, I could comb it myself. I only had one concern, that the boys would still like me without long hair.

For the first week of school, I couldn't do any work because my special typewriter hadn't arrived. Instead, I sat at a small table at the back of the classroom and watched.

When my typewriter finally arrived, the teacher moved my table to one side of the room near an electrical outlet. After the machine was plugged in, I remember all eyes upon me as I lifted

Me at 11 years of age with a pixie cut (1967). I was worried that the boys wouldn't like me with short hair.

the lid. And when I started to type, my classmates couldn't help gathering around.

For many days every member of the class was more interested in my typewriter than doing schoolwork. As usual, I enjoyed the attention. After a few weeks, though, the excitement of having an electric typewriter in the classroom wore off.

I soon developed a system for doing each assignment. In Math I used my typewriter to write numbers in vertical rows. Most reading assignments were in workbooks, so I simply typed my answers onto a separate sheet of paper. For Social Studies, Science and Spelling lessons, I was able to copy from the blackboard as long as I was given extra time.

I was surprised at how well I got along. I even started to use both hands to type. I'd rest my palms on either side of the typewriter and hit the keys with my two index fingers, relying mostly on the right one. I could usually manage to type about three words out of five without making a mistake, but sometimes my hands would spasm and I'd hit four or five keys at once, causing them to jam. Still, compared to writing by hand, typing was pretty easy. The only thing that worried me was disturbing others with my tap-tap-tapping.

My parents did their best to help me with homework. Nita helped, too, especially with Math. If Mom and Dad were too busy to help, I'd get upset and yell. Then a fight would start, usually with Mom, and our language would get pretty foul. When that happened, Dad would step in, and Mom and I would shut up. Dad had become very opposed to swearing and arguing since joining the Mormon Church. For this reason, I usually got the help I needed, just to keep peace in the family.

Things as an eleven-year-old grade four student were going along fairly well until I started to hang around with a few grade sevens, a group that used to smoke on the way home from school.

One day these kids offered me a cigarette, but as I tried to light it, it broke in two. They got a big laugh out of that. Then we discovered that if someone lit the cigarette for me, I could manage the rest.

On weekends, we'd all chip in to buy a package of 'smokes.' We'd sit in a secluded spot behind McDougall Pool puffing to our hearts' content. However, I soon found out that smoking put a huge dent in my weekly allowance.

One of the grade sevens revealed an easier way to get smokes. At the Super Value grocery store, packs were stacked next to the checkout counters. The last counter next to the exit doors was hardly ever used. If you played your cards just right and strolled by when nobody was watching the last counter, you could grab a couple of packs, put them in your pocket and walk out.

So, one day two of my grade seven friends and I left school during the lunch hour to try out this plan. First we wandered around the store, getting up our nerve. Then they chose me to do the dirty work. Unfortunately, as I made my way to the last counter it was suddenly opened for customers.

Even though my first thought was to forget the smokes, I carried on by changing the plan. I pretended to become interested in some chocolate bars displayed next to the cigarettes. In no time, a few people had squeezed ahead of me and I had my chance. I made sure the cashier wasn't looking. Then, with my more coordinated right hand, I managed to grab two packs of Number 7's and stuff them into the right pocket of my coat. Next, I picked up an Oh Henry bar with the same hand and pretended to inspect it as I nervously got into line.

Before long, the cashier was kindly looking at me. I knew that Mom always put a dime in the left pocket of my coat in case I needed money for a phone call, probably thinking that in the left pocket it'd be a little tougher for me to get out and spend. *How am I going to get that dime out?* I thought.

I was scared stiff as I began fumbling my way into my left coat pocket with my shaky left hand. The cashier waited patiently for a while and then made a move to help me.

"No-I ... got-it," I said. And a moment later I really did feel the dime pinched in my palm. I pulled out my hand with a jerk and dropped it onto the counter.

As the cashier picked it up, I relaxed a little; I was still shaking with fear, but luckily the woman couldn't tell that I was shaking more than I usually did. She smiled a thank-you, and I walked out.

My friends met me in the parking lot and I showed off the two packs of Lucky 7's. I had already begun to feel guilty for my crime, but these feelings soon disappeared when my friends started congratulating me for a job well done.

Soon, stealing cigarettes became a regular routine for the three of us. We took turns 'swiping smokes' and I used my chocolate bar trick whenever the last checkout was occupied.

One day when it was my turn to do the swiping, I decided to show off. The last checkout was unoccupied, so I went straight to it, picked up a pack of smokes and, keeping them in my right hand, boldly carried on through the exit doors.

I stepped into the parking lot, smiling at my friends, but right away I noticed that they weren't smiling back. Instead, they looked scared. I turned around and saw a woman running toward me. My friends then took off like wild rabbits. I took off, too. I ran the best I could through the parking lot and made it across the street before the woman caught hold of my coat. I had placed the pack of smokes under my left arm, but that didn't fool her.

"Aren't you forgetting to pay for something?" she said, pulling the cigarette pack from its hiding place. "I think you'd better come with me!"

As she escorted me back to the store, horrible thoughts were going through my head. The police station was across the street, and I was sure I'd be spending the night in a prison cell.

The woman presented me to the store manager and said, "I caught her stealing cigarettes."

They talked for a while, deciding what to do. Then the

woman, who was standing behind me, said, "Maybe we should let her go because ...."

I glanced her way and looked up. She was tapping her forefingers on her temples. I knew what that meant. She was saying that I was mentally retarded and didn't know any better. Her suggestion got me mad. I wanted to scream out: "I am not retarded! I'm as smart as any other kid my age!" I felt the same way I always felt when someone made fun of me. But I remained silent. Under the circumstances, it was wiser for me to let them think what they wanted.

"You can go," the manager said. "Don't let it happen again or we'll call the police next time."

That experience scared my friends and me enough to make us stop stealing cigarettes. From then on we smoked a lot less, only what our weekly allowances could buy. It was just as well for me. Because of my operation, the glands in my cheeks would swell up and hurt if I smoked too much.

ஸ்ஓ ஓஸ்

For some reason, just before the Christmas vacation, I found myself in a nasty mood. I was at school playing with two girls from my new class, and I suggested we pick on some girls from Mrs. Baglot's class. One of the girls had been my best friend the year before.

We told them they were in the 'stupid class,' they were the 'dumbest kids in the school,' and even that they were 'retarded.'

For several days, words came out of my mouth that I'd always hated hearing. We'd chase and torment our victims, yelling nonstop insults at them. It felt good to harass them.

But before the week was out, my teacher approached me during Math and told me to report to Mrs. Baglot immediately.

When I walked into my old classroom, every eye was focused on me. Mrs. Baglot sat at her desk and ordered me to the front of the class, and as I squirmed she told the class what my friends and I had been doing.

Her final words really hurt: "I'm shocked that you of all people would do such a thing. You're the last one who should talk such nonsense; you were in this class last year and know these kids are as smart as anyone else. And now you torment a girl who used to be your friend? You should be ashamed of yourself!"

When Mrs. Baglot had finished speaking, I fully realized that what I had been doing was wrong. Still, I couldn't admit it. Instead, I burst into tears, hoping that Mrs. Baglot would see I was sorry and let me return to my classroom.

She didn't give in: "Crying like a baby isn't going to help you, Nova."

Finally, I wiped away my tears and admitted, "I-don'-know … why-I … did-it. I'm sor-ry." Then the lunch bell rang.

"You can go, that's all for now," she said. I had never seen her so disappointed in me.

Before I left, I apologized again to my old classmate, and her smile told me that she forgave me.

⁕

As I approached my twelfth birthday, I began to think more than ever about the opposite sex. I'd had a few romances in Mrs. Baglot's class, but since moving on it seemed that all the boys I knew were just good friends, nothing more. I liked to gossip about boys with my girlfriends and discuss their romances, but I didn't have a boyfriend of my own.

It didn't take long before I started to feel that my handicap was the only reason I didn't have a boyfriend. *Who wants to go around with a girl who shakes and walks like a drunk?* I'd think. I started to feel hateful, and as though I'd never be as attractive as other girls in Kimberley.

One night I was brooding about this in my bedroom, and it made me so upset I began to sob hysterically. My mother peeked in to see what was up and I took my anger out on her. I worked myself up into a temper tantrum and screamed, "Boys ... hate-me! It's-your-fault ... I'm ... like-this! YOU ... made-me-this ... way!"

Usually, Mom would put up a pretty good fight. But this time when she heard my words she quietly left the room. Later, as I sat on my bed, I could hear her crying in the living room.

After a fight, my mother and I always made up. I felt terrible because I knew I had hurt her more than ever before, so I crept downstairs and sheepishly joined her on the couch.

When her tears let up, she said, "Nova, you'll always have CP. You'll never lose it and you can't hide it. It's not a sickness you'll grow out of. It's part of you." We cuddled, and Mom rocked me for a little while before adding, "As for boys, you're too young to worry about them. One day, you'll meet a nice young man. Wait until you're older. You'll see. You'll get the best."

CHAPTER 11

I was nervous as grade four came to a close. *Would I pass?* I wondered. I had turned twelve, so I was getting a little old for the fourth grade. Furthermore, I wanted to move on with my classmates. Even though I had been teased and misunderstood once in a while, I had made many new friends who knew I could think as well as they could; and even the few kids who had a tough time accepting me knew I had normal intelligence.

On the last day of school, the last line of my report card told the story: Assigned to Grade 5. I had done well enough in each subject to pass – no B's or A's, but I hadn't failed.

A normal summer to look forward to, two months of holidays free of Children's Hospital, would have made the end of school seem even sweeter. But of course my yearly stay in Vancouver was just around the corner.

Staying at Children's Hospital was again going to be difficult, but for a different reason. My mother, father and Nita were planning a six-week vacation in the United States. Some of the highlights of their trip would be Disneyland, Las Vegas and Salt Lake City.

I envisioned being shut up in Children's Hospital and

receiving postcards saying what a great time they were having. And I knew that when I got back from the hospital, Nita would tease me endlessly about all the fun I'd missed.

There was a slim chance, however, that I'd be able to join my family on their trip. Each year the hospital sent an official letter with the details of my summer program. It was possible that I wouldn't receive the letter because the postal workers were on the verge of striking.

"If we don't hear from the hospital before the strike, you'll be coming with us. Let's keep our fingers crossed," Mom said.

However, a few days before the Canada Post Strike of 1968 was scheduled to happen, a large envelope from Children's Hospital arrived. Mom and I were the only ones home that morning, and when she showed me the envelope she could see my spirits sink. She opened it and said, "It looks like they want you for another full summer of therapy."

"It's-not … fair!" I screamed, and I started to cry.

At that my mother did something that startled me. She tore up the letter and threw it into our wood stove. "As far as anyone is going to know, it didn't come. We'll blame it on the strike. Let's just leave it at that. You're coming with us."

For the first time since beginning my yearly stays in Vancouver I was going to have a summer holiday – no doctors or nurses, no therapists or therapy, no hospitals or rehab centers.

I started telling everyone I knew that I was going to Disneyland. Nita couldn't figure out how I was so sure I wasn't going to Children's Hospital.

"Jus … wait … an-see!" I'd tell her.

Meanwhile, Mom and I were the only ones who knew the truth.

Mom, Dad, Nita and I began our trip by stopping off in Nelson for a short visit with Flo and her family. She was heavy with her third child, which was due in August. The baby would be born about the time we returned.

We then headed straight for the border. Once we were across, Dad drove almost non-stop until we reached California.

Just a few days after we left Kimberley, we were in Hollywood, driving down Sunset Boulevard, and I was on the lookout for movie stars.

Traveling to California to visit Disneyland had seemed like an impossibility just weeks beforehand. Finding myself there, I was constantly wanting to shriek with excitement. However, Dad had to concentrate on driving, so I contained myself.

Before we got to see Disneyland, we stayed with Dad's nephew who lived in Los Angeles. He and his wife had three children, a boy who was a year older than me and four-year-old twin girls.

It didn't take long before my cousins were asking embarrassing questions like: "Why does she walk like that?" and "Why does she talk like she has rocks in her mouth?"

It took a lot of explaining from my parents and their parents to help them begin to understand my handicap. Still, the little girls looked at me oddly – as though they were waiting for me to do something really strange like throw one of them out the window.

We said good-bye to our California relatives a few days later and finally headed for Disneyland. I remember it taking forever to get there, and parking the car and making our way across the parking lot to the entrance took just as long.

Then, at last, we were through the gates and entering what

seemed a dream world! Everywhere I looked there was some kind of castle or fantastic building.

The first attraction that lured us in was an immense room full of stuffed exotic birds. When everyone was seated, the lights went out and thousands of multi-coloured lights flashed on bringing the birds to life. They sang and danced and flitted about as though they were real. I fantasized standing up and dancing with them, but something told me that if I did the birds might get upset.

I remember too sitting down for a while and listening to Mickey Mouse's children, a group of kids who sang many of my favourite songs. When I was bored in school, I used to daydream about being a singer in Hollywood movies or a stage performer. When we played records at home, I'd pretend I had a microphone in my hand and move my lips as though I was singing. When I heard good music, I had to dance. I had the urge to do just that as I sat listening to those Disney songs.

Other highlights of our day included the Jungle Cruise and the Matterhorn.

During the Jungle Cruise, I hung on to Mom in case I had a spasm; I didn't want to fall in the water and be devoured by one of the mechanical yawning hippos or some other underwater creature I couldn't see.

All day Nita and I had looked forward to the Matterhorn, a sensational roller coaster ride that streaked up and down and through a life-like mountain. After waiting in line for an hour, a man stopped Nita and I before we could get on. He looked at me uncertainly and then asked Nita if she was sure I'd be all right. She assured him I'd be okay, and he reluctantly helped us into a coaster car. It sure didn't take long before I was wishing the operator had kept me off the ride. Once we had climbed to the top of the mountain and were on our way down, we moved incredibly fast, too fast for me! I clung hard to the bar on my side of the car, closed my eyes and buried my face in one arm. Nita kept yelling at me to relax and enjoy the swirling dips and free falls, but I couldn't. I was sure that if I relaxed my grip even the least little bit I'd fall out.

Before leaving Disneyland, we saw the Mickey Mouse Parade with its marching bands and floats, and then the most spectacular fireworks I had ever seen.

After the fireworks, as we walked through the gates and away, I felt a little sad. My CP had seemed less of a big deal at Disneyland and now it was back to the real world. I trudged along quietly while everyone else complained about their sore feet.

Once we left Disneyland, Dad drove late into the night toward our next two destinations, Las Vegas and Salt Lake City. After a short rest in a motel and a long drive, mostly through desert lands, we arrived in the evening in Las Vegas. The city was impressive at night. Millions of colourful lights would almost blind you no matter where you looked. But otherwise, Las Vegas didn't interest me much.

I soon figured out that Las Vegas was a kind of Disneyland for adults. There was entertainment galore for them – gambling, stage shows, concerts and fancy restaurants – but not much for kids to do.

Mom and Dad gambled while we were there. The more I watched them and thousands of others gamble, the more confused I became. It seemed a crazy thing to do. Sometimes I'd see a slot machine or card table pay off, but mostly I watched frustrated people lose their money.

I was glad when we left Las Vegas and were on our way to Salt Lake City. I was looking forward to swimming in the salty lake there. I had heard that because of all the salt it was impossible to sink. I thought, *This will be my chance to swim without worrying about drowning.*

Of course we were also visiting Salt Lake City because we had become Mormons. We were keen to see the Mormon Temple there, the headquarters of our church. My Sunday school teacher had told us how the entire structure was built without a single nail. We all thought it would be fantastic to see the real thing.

We spent one week sightseeing in and around Salt Lake City. We toured the Mormon Temple and Brigham Young's house and heard the Mormon Tabernacle Choir, but I never did swim in the Great Salt Lake. I ended up catching a cold, and Mom wouldn't let me in the water!

When we finally arrived back in Kimberley, we found a huge pile of mail waiting for us. Amongst the mail was another envelope from Children's Hospital. A letter inside said it was their second attempt to contact us, and they "would regret it very much" if I couldn't show up for my "annual visit."

Dad was puzzled about what had happened to the first letter. Mom just shrugged her shoulders. Then she turned around to me and winked.

CHAPTER 12

As grade five unfolded, I began to realize why Mom wasn't too concerned about my missed visit to Children's Hospital. I sensed – and she must have known – that my visits there were coming to an end.

After all, my handicap wasn't hindering me too much in school, and my drooling was under control. My problems were manageable except for the teasing I endured, and physical therapy could do nothing to help that.

Sure enough, early the following summer of 1969, when we travelled to Vancouver I was only in Children's Hospital for three days, just long enough for a thorough check-up. The doctors seemed the most interested in the operation that had been performed on my saliva glands, and after many of them had looked me over, they declared that it had been a success. They also told my parents that more therapy wouldn't help me enough to justify further visits.

One of them said, "I'm sorry, Mr. and Mrs. Bannatyne, but there are many other disabled children who need these services."

I didn't mind at all. A few months after my thirteenth birthday, news that I was being freed for another summer was music to my ears!

Soon after we got home from Vancouver, I started pestering my parents to let me have a bike. I'd dreamed of riding my own bike ever since Jeannie had doubled me around on hers years before.

I was always trying to ride my friends' bikes. At first I could only go a few feet before falling off. But I kept practicing every chance I had until I could ride quite a distance without toppling over or shaking the handlebars too much. Riding in the streets made me nervous, but I could go for long rides in McDougall Park where there was lots of grass if I fell.

My parents didn't believe me when I told them that I had learned to ride a bike, so one day I borrowed Maxine's Mustang and took it home. Mom and Dad watched in disbelief as I rode up and down our driveway. Before long both of them were clapping wildly for me, as though I had just won a relay race.

A couple of weekends later, Dad took me downtown to look for a used bike.

"I-wann'-a … good-one," I told him as we left the house on foot. "Let's-use … my sav-ings."

So we went to the Credit Union first, where I took out $58.00. Six dollars was from collecting pop bottles and the rest was money my relatives had given me after Jeannie's funeral.

Soon after, in a cycling shop I loved to go into I spotted the bike I wanted right away, a used blue Mustang with a white banana seat, white handle grips and white-walled tires. But it was $65.00.

Dad agreed to pitch in the extra seven dollars to buy it, but he insisted on looking it over very carefully first to make sure it was in good shape. After what seemed forever, he said, "Looks ship shape, let's buy it."

When Dad wheeled that Mustang out of the shop, I followed so closely he could barely manage the thing.

"I-can't-be-lieve … its-mine," I said, looking up at him.

As soon as we had put a little extra air in the tires, he escorted me to McDougall Park, and I rode on to see if I could find Nita or any of our friends.

Having a bike added even more freedom to my second summer away from Children's Hospital. And even though it went by quickly, it was one of the best summers ever. When I wasn't hanging around McDougall Pool, I rode my bike day and night.

⚬⚬⚬ ⚬⚬⚬

The kids who congregated at the pool were a pretty tough bunch, but there was an older boy I liked named Wayne. He was friendly and never called me names or mocked me. My friends and I had a bit of a crush on him.

The summer I got my bike Wayne and I hung around a lot. The other kids started calling us sweethearts, but we were just friends. We'd sit in the park and talk together for hours, and sometimes we'd go swimming. If people insinuated anything about us, Wayne would swear at them or threaten to beat them up.

Wayne was one of the few people I ever talked to about my handicap. I remember him asking: "How do you eat?" and "How do you deal with the jerks that call you retard or shaky gimp?"

I hated lying to someone who was so nice to me, but after his first question I said, "I-jus'-eat … ver-y … slow-ly." I was too embarrassed to say that the easiest thing was for my mother or someone else to spoon-feed me. As for dealing with my tormentors, I said, "I-jus'-get-away. I-can-move … fast-er now-that-I-have … a-bike."

"Well," he replied, "as far as I care you're the same as any other kid around here: you swim, you ride a bike, you swear sometimes, and you've got a reputation for being tough."

I think he respected me because I did what I wanted in spite of my handicap. In his eyes I was an equal.

One thing I *can't* thank Wayne for is teaching me how to smoke. I didn't realize that when I had smoked before, I had never inhaled. Wayne taught me how to take a drag, breathe in the smoke, and then blow it out. "You gotta get the nicotine," he'd say. It didn't take long before I was hooked.

I remember well the first smoke Wayne and I shared. I did as he showed me, and after coughing a few times I got the hang of it. I felt fine at first, but when I stood up I felt dizzy. Then I collapsed on the grass and started throwing up. I felt as though I was dying! As I lay with my face in the grass, I could hear Wayne roaring with laughter.

The next day, my face swelled up like a balloon. I swore I'd never touch another cigarette, but of course it didn't take long before I was right back at it.

When Wayne wasn't around, I tried to avoid the kids I knew would tease me, especially the ones who said it looked hilarious when I smoked. If I craved nicotine, I'd first have to find a place to hide before I could light my cigarette.

Lighting up was hard. I had to lie on my stomach and set a cigarette and an open pack of matches on the grass, then strike and hold a match with my right hand, pick up the cigarette with my lips, and finally guide the match to the end of it.

Nine times out of ten, I'd break the cigarette or get it too wet or the match would go out because my hand was too shaky. I knew that the whole procedure looked awfully funny, so I did my best to make sure nobody saw me.

When I smoked with Wayne, he'd light up for me and gingerly place the cigarette between my fingers. He had to be careful, though, because if I had even a slight spasm the cigarette would either burn one of us or rip apart.

Everywhere I went that summer I rode my bike. I pedaled to the park, the pool, the school grounds and friends' homes. I quickly got over my fear of riding on streets, but I was still nervous on hills and avoided them whenever possible.

After church on Sundays, I'd go off on long bike rides with another good friend named Cathy. We usually ended up at the park on the swings, but sometimes we'd ride to the graveyard.

Cathy's sister had died as an infant, so we'd look at her grave and, of course, at Jeannie's.

Whenever we visited the graveyard, I felt sad. Even after three years, I missed Jeannie a lot. I'd have given anything to have her back.

⚬ஃ ஃ⚬

One Sunday near the end of the summer Cathy didn't want to ride with me. So I took off by myself.

I rode around downtown more confidently than usual because there wasn't much traffic in Kimberley on Sundays. I eventually made my way to McDougall Park and watched a softball game. Actually, I remember only half-watching that game because I was too busy keeping an eye on my bike. I had laid it down on some grass just off the pavement of a nearby parking lot.

Near the end of the ball game, I noticed a car full of teenagers recklessly backing up in the parking lot.

No!-Stop!" I screamed when I realized they were headed straight for my bike.

But the driver of the car didn't stop until he'd backed right over it. The sound of crunching metal stunned me and choked off my screams. Dad had just bought a carrying basket, and it was the last thing I heard being flattened.

The driver opened his door, glanced backwards with a smirk, then slammed the door shut and drove forward, running over my bike a second time! The car then screeched out of the parking lot, and I could see heads bobbing around inside, like everyone was having a good laugh.

"I-bet … they-knew … it-was-mine," I muttered tearfully as I made my way to the scene of the crime.

When I got to where my bike lay, I stood it up, hoping it wasn't too badly damaged. But the spokes on both tires were broken, the handlebars were twisted and the front sprocket was so badly bent that I couldn't get the chain back on.

As I added up the damage, tears began to pour out of my eyes.

A good fifteen minutes later, while I was still standing there sobbing, a car pulled up in front of me and a man got out. It was our neighbour, Ronnie and Brian's dad. "Calm down, Nova," he said, placing a hand on my shoulder.

Once I had contained my tears, he lifted my bike into the trunk of his car, handling it as though it was an injured animal he was taking to the vet.

When I arrived home with my broken bike, my parents were relaxing on the front porch and had little sympathy for me.

Mom said, "You should've parked it more safely."

"You'll have to save up your allowance again if you want it fixed," said Dad.

Then they went in the house with me crying on the front steps and my bike in a pathetic heap on the sidewalk at my feet.

It wasn't long, though, before I saw Nita walking toward me. Ronnie and Brian accompanied her. Ronnie was carrying a toolbox, and shouted, "Get ready, Nova! You're going to help us put this bike back together."

I thought, *If this bike can be fixed, Ronnie and Brian can do it!* From the time Nita and I were little, they'd come to our rescue many times, fixing our broken toys with their tools.

For a skinny guy, Ronnie was pretty strong. In a flash, he pulled the handlebars back into place. Then Brian took the tires off, removed the broken spokes and straightened the bent ones. "There are too many spokes here anyway, Nova; a few less won't hurt," he joked.

In awe, Nita and I stood nearby watching and occasionally handed them the tools they needed.

In a few hours my bike looked almost as good as new!

Even though my bike looked great to me, I was forbidden to ride it.

"That thing isn't safe," declared Dad. "I don't want you riding to school until it's fixed properly. Winter will be here soon, anyways. If you've saved enough by spring or summer to get it fixed, you can ride it then."

I was heartbroken. I had so looked forward to riding that bike, my pride and joy, to school.

CHAPTER 13

ﾟ๏ﾟ ๑ﾟ๑

September meant school supplies, a brand new outfit and early mornings once again.

I loved getting ready for school, but I had begun to hate following Nita there. My mother and sister often got annoyed with me because I'd refuse to head out if anyone, even someone who knew me well, was on the sidewalk.

"Go on," Mom would say. "They're not going to tease you. They won't even notice you."

I didn't care what Mom said. I preferred to wait until the street was empty so that no one would see how I moved.

When the coast was clear. Nita would charge out the door and I'd break into a lopsided gallop behind her. I always felt better practicing running without an audience.

ﾟ๏ﾟ ๑ﾟ๑

I was determined to take grade six seriously, and I started off doing well. I never became a "goody-goody," but I liked my teacher and wanted him to like me, so I worked hard.

After the first month, however, I slipped into some bad habits. Most of the kids who sat at the back with me were pretty rowdy. They swore a lot and loved to bother our teacher, and I began to follow their lead.

Swearing wasn't new to me. I had been swearing ever since I had discovered that it made other kids laugh. It didn't take long before I was swearing and talking back to our teacher, too.

My classmates got a charge out of my antics, and I got the positive attention I craved. My teacher, Mr. Kay, knew exactly how to handle me and used his sense of humour to turn me around.

Mr. Kay was a tall, skinny man with black hair, and he spoke very softly, with an Australian accent. We thought it was hilarious when he said things like 'nought' instead of 'zero.' But when we laughed at him, he could always see the joke and laugh along with us.

Once he gave us a lecture on the differences between his way of speaking and ours. When he had finished, I said, "Gee, Mr.-Kay ... I-thought-you ... were ... talking- that-way ... just-to-make-me ... feel good." For a few moments, his face went beet red with embarrassment. Then he realized I was joking and we all had a good laugh.

Whenever Mr. Kay caught me chatting or joking with my classmates, he never lost his sense of humour as he got me back on track, even if I got the last word, which I usually did.

"Nova," he said one day as I tried to engage a few friends in conversation, "would you please quit talking to that electric typewriter and listen? If you'd be quiet for a minute, maybe that thing could rest its ears while you learn something." He knew this remark would amuse the class.

"But Mr.-Kay," I answered, "if-I-don't-talk ... to-my-machine

... it'll-fall-asleep ... and-I'll-never-get-any-thing ... done." As usual, I got the last laugh that day.

In spite of my behaviour, Mr. Kay gave me a lot of individual attention and found new ways of helping me with my work.

In Math, he understood my difficulties right away. He could see how bored I was typing out the problems before solving them, so he copied them out for me. "All you have to do is fill in the numbers and come up with the right answers," he'd say.

Almost every day after school, I'd wait for about fifteen minutes while Mr. Kay created worksheets for me. He made sure that I had no excuses for not doing my Math homework.

In Science we used various kinds of apparatus such as expensive microscopes, as well as glass slides that I found impossible to handle. Whenever I tried to place a tiny specimen on a slide, my hands would jerk and send the slide and specimen flying. A few times I even knocked over the microscope.

I thought my problems were solved when Mr. Kay divided the class into teams of four. Other people prepared the slide with the specimen and stain, put the slide in place and got the microscope focused for viewing.

But I even had trouble looking through the lens because I couldn't hold my head still. As I tried to bring my eye toward the microscope, my head would jerk and bang against it; or even worse, I'd sometimes get close but then poke my eye right into the eyepiece.

Good old Mr. Kay didn't give up. He directed my teammates to take turns holding and steadying my head as I looked through the lens. It was the only solution.

In the spring, around the time I turned fourteen, I noticed that many of the eleven and twelve-year-old girls in my class were beginning to wear bras. Even though I was a couple of years older, my breasts weren't big enough to need one. Still, I wondered how a bra would feel. I used to talk about this and other things with Cathy.

Once I noticed that she had hair under her arms, and I teased her, saying she looked like a hairy monkey. She told me that I had hairy armpits, too. It surprised me because I hadn't noticed.

We then began talking about menstruation, and Cathy said she'd started her periods when she was ten. That also surprised me because I hadn't started yet. So when she asked me about my periods, I told her mine started when I was nine. I didn't want to seem backward and was afraid that she'd think it had something to do with my handicap.

I felt better though when the health nurse showed us a film on the topic. It said menstruation could start as early as eight and as late as seventeen. My time just hadn't come, I figured.

Sometimes Cathy or some other girl in Mr. Kay's class would ask me to stay overnight. The prospect always made me nervous because I hated strangers seeing how I handled a knife and fork, and I feared making a mess on someone else's furniture or floors.

This was a problem on trips away from home too, but during those times it was always solved by my mother feeding me.

So when I did stay the night at a friend's house I tried to avoid eating with the family. A piece of toast at breakfast was the most I could manage without embarrassment.

I was a little sad when my year with Mr. Kay came to an end. He had worked hard to understand me and make adaptations for my handicap. I knew I had made great strides forward as a learner, all because of him.

As summer began, my sadness was soothed by the fact that my bike was almost back on the road. I had been able to save enough to fix it properly, and it was just about ready to be picked up from the shop.

Early in July it was back in my hands, and I remember my Dad saying, "Don't forget, it's now a $75.00 bike. Look after it."

The summer of 1970 there was a big change at home. For all of July and August, Nita went to live with Flo and help her look after our three nephews.

Nita was especially excited because Flo's youngest son was out of diapers and walking and talking like mad. Furthermore, she was looking forward to traveling a bit further from home. Flo and Stewart had moved from Nelson to Lethbridge, Alberta.

Life wasn't quite the same without Nita around. She and her gang were no longer there to help keep the bullies who teased me in line. And home was different without a sister to talk to or fight with. I still had the occasional fight with Mom, but that was never as much fun as fighting with Nita.

Even though I had lots of friends in town, I ended up spending much more time alone. I'd sometimes watch TV with my parents and talk to them, but still I became more and more unhappy. And, with Nita not around, I ended up riding my bike a lot less than I thought I would.

I was free from Children's Hospital for another summer, but I was lonely.

Then one day in late July some neighbours invited me in to see some puppies they were hoping to give away, and I immediately

Mickey and me in our backyard.
He was a true friend, loving me unconditionally.

fell in love with one. He was a fighter! He'd push past the others
to nurse and enjoyed tussling with his brothers and sisters.

After a few visits I convinced myself that I had to have that
dog. I even had a name ready for him, Mickey. So I spoke up for
Mickey, even though I hadn't yet asked my parents.

I kept visiting Mickey every day for a couple of weeks, and
as I watched him grow, I fell more and more in love with him.

When the time came to take Mickey home, I first had to break the news to my parents. I remember pleading with them: "Dogs-are ... good-for-me ... because-they treat-me ... like-a-friend ... they-never tease-me ... they-never hurt-me ... they-never leave-me ... a-lone." I said this with real tears in my eyes, which made it hard for my parents to refuse.

Mom gave in first, saying, "Your allowance will have to go towards caring for him; there won't be any left for much else."

And Dad said, "You'd better make sure you give him enough attention so he doesn't bother the rest of us."

The summer holidays became more tolerable once I brought Mickey home.

At first I spent hours just watching the little guy because I was a bit nervous to handle him. *I might drop or hurt him if I have a spasm*, I thought.

I was surprised that I seldom had a spasm as I held Mickey, and even if I did, it was never violent enough to put him in danger.

When I wasn't watching or playing with Mickey, I was making sure he was fed or taken outside to do his business. It was also a lot of fun teaching him to follow as I rode my bike.

We were steadfast companions for the rest of the summer.

∾ଓଓ ଓଚ∾

In spite of the joy Mickey brought into my life, I was happy when summer was over and Nita returned home for the start of school.

Nita moved on to junior high school that year, but I didn't mind. The most important thing was that she was home again.

CHAPTER 14

G rade seven got off to a rocky start. My main teacher seemed like a nice enough fellow at first. He liked to kid around like Mr. Kay, and since he was a little crippled himself (he had one leg shorter than the other and walked with a limp), I thought we were going to understand each other.

One day he asked each person in the class to read a paragraph from the text out loud. He went person by person down each row giving everyone a turn. When he came to me, however, he passed by and went to the next person.

John, who had been in my classes since grade four, called out: "Hey, you missed Nova."

"Never mind," he said, speaking up so the whole class could hear, "she'd read too slowly, and we wouldn't understand her."

"But we could follow her in our books," replied Donna, a girl who was new to the school and Kimberley.

"Carry on reading," he said to the boy sitting behind me.

At that I felt nothing but intense hatred for this teacher. He was denying my right to equal treatment. None of my former teachers had ever been so rude and unfeeling. I wanted to slam my book shut and walk out of the room. But instead I remained silent and kept my eyes down. I looked at my book – but I saw nothing.

Fortunately, I had other teachers that year who were kinder.

My Health teacher didn't hesitate to tell me how much she respected the way I handled myself. Just by the way she looked at me, she always gave me the feeling that I was brave and intelligent. Every now and then she'd give me a big smile and say words like, "Set your goals high, Nova! Work hard towards them, and I know you'll get what you want out of life."

I also got along well with my Science teacher, the vice-principal. He had a reputation for being mean and tough, but he liked me and somehow I became his favourite. He always made sure I had enough time to copy from the blackboard, and if I was still having trouble keeping up, he'd place his own master notes next to my typewriter. When he graded our notebooks, mine always came back with a huge A or B in red marking pencil.

I liked my Social Studies teacher, too, but every time I entered his classroom, I'd recall an embarrassing event.

When I was in grade six, I stopped by his door and looked in because I recognized my cousin, Bob. "Bobtail" and I had been great playmates as little kids.

He didn't know I was there until someone said, "Hey, Bob, there's your retarded cousin!"

He then turned around red-faced and gave me a quick wave as if to say: "Hi, bye!"

Not long into the school year, I had an encounter with my old smoking buddy, Wayne, which changed our friendship for awhile. I had seen him around town during the summer, but we hardly spent any time together – not like the previous summer. He was always busy socializing or on his way somewhere. Even though he'd often toss me a cigarette, he'd say things like "Gotta' get goin', Nova" or "I'll see ya' later."

One day as I was making my way home through the school grounds I noticed Wayne approaching with Colin, our Student Council president. Colin was one of the few people who still had to remind me regularly of my awkwardness.

As we passed one another, Colin began mumbling like his mouth was full of jaw breakers, and he made his legs stiff and waved his hands around.

Even worse, Wayne copied him and threw in some extra abuse. "Hey, retard! Hey, spastic! Are you drunk?" he taunted, and they both laughed.

I felt like crying on the spot but decided I wouldn't give them the satisfaction. I gave them the dirtiest look I could muster instead.

However, as soon as I glared at Wayne, he spat at me. He missed, but the act hurt more than any words could.

At that point I wanted to slap Wayne's face. I held off, though, because I was afraid he'd beat me up. Then he and his pal walked on without looking back.

I hurried home and found Mom sitting in her favourite chair watching TV.

"Hi, Nova, you're home a little earlier than usual. This is nice for a change. As soon as Nita and your dad get home we'll eat." The way Mom spoke told me she was in a good mood.

I wanted to answer like I was in a good mood, too, but all that came out was, "I'm-not-really … that-hungry, Mom."

Me not being hungry was all my mother needed to let her know that something was wrong.

"Did something go wrong at school today? Did you get into trouble?" she questioned with kindness, not anger, in her voice.

"Nothing ... happened-at-school ... but after-school ... something-did," I said, and I could feel my tears coming.

"Kids teasing you again? You shouldn't listen to them." Mom's voice was still kind and tender.

I broke down, I couldn't help it, and through tears explained the whole episode on the school grounds.

First Mom hugged me, and then said, "Oh, Nova, Wayne was just acting like a big shot to impress his friend. That's the way people are sometimes; they have to hurt somebody else to make themselves look big. Someday Wayne will come around, and I bet he'll even say he is sorry."

A lot of what Mom said was true. While I had witnessed Wayne bullying people to look tough, one-on-one as you got to know him he could be super nice. He had listening ears and an understanding heart.

Still, I secretly vowed that even if he did apologize I'd spit at him and call him the dirtiest name that popped into my head.

Occasionally on weekends our family would travel to Lethbridge to visit Flo, Stewart and their three boys.

Nita was close to Stewart Jr., Johnny and Chris, because she had looked after them every summer of their lives. I, on the other hand, had missed out on getting close because I'd spent so many summers at Children's Hospital. Also, because of my handicap, Flo always seemed a little nervous when I was around the children. Still, I was very fond of all three boys and wished I could see more of them.

I had wonderful memories of Stewart Jr. as a baby (when there was no prejudice in his heart). He'd cuddle up to me as we watched TV, and when I took him for walks, he clutched my hand and wouldn't let go. Those times I loved the little guy like crazy.

As he grew older, though, there were times when he hurt my feelings. For example, during one of our visits to Lethbridge, he imitated the way I struggled with my spoon as I ate, mocking my frustration. I knew he was too young to understand how such acts hurt me, but I still felt embarrassed and annoyed.

It seemed that the older I got, the more I avoided young children, especially those I didn't know.

At Flo's, if she asked me to come along with her and the boys to the park or store, I'd get a queasy feeling in my stomach. Knowing we were going to such places meant there was no way I could avoid staring eyes and cruel taunts.

I remember that one time when we visited Flo, Nita took me next door to visit a girl named Audrey. The two had become best friends over the course of many summers. The house seemed to have wall-to-wall kids, from age two to eighteen. As I entered, they all gathered around and stared at me as though I was some kind of freak. I never went back!

Another time, some of Flo and Stewart's friends came over with their youngsters. Soon after the little ones saw me, they were asking questions ("Why does she walk so funny?" "Why can't she talk like us?" "Why can't she eat normally?"). They'd stay close to their mother, as if I was a creature from the planet Mars that any second might snatch them for an early dinner.

Luckily, I could usually turn to my mother for comfort and compassion. Because nobody else since Jeannie understood me better, Mom and I seemed to spend lots of time together, especially during the winter.

Mom was miserable when the cold weather hit. She couldn't get into the garden and my father was so involved with sports that he was out most evenings. So when Nita would head out too, I'd stay home and keep her company.

We usually just watched TV, but sometimes we'd play Crazy Eights. This card game helped to pass the time, but it also provided an opportunity to talk.

Mom had some fascinating stories about her childhood in Holland during World War II. Because my grandfather was Jewish, her family had experienced some difficult times.

Once her older brother went out to buy bread and after a couple of hours hadn't returned. My grandfather went out to search and found his son lying wounded in the street. The Germans had shot him in the leg and left him to die. Luckily, he survived.

When Mom told me such stories, her face was full of fear and sorrow. I'd feel closer to her at these times, because I understood that her own childhood wasn't always happy.

⁖⊙℘ ℘⊙⁖

As my grade seven year came successfully to a close, it was my mother who was most proud. Overall, I had done well. My marks were mostly above average and my teachers had praised me for good work habits. As Mom read my final report card, tears filled her eyes. "I am so proud of you, Nova," she said. "I hope you'll always work hard. If you do, you'll always do well. Stay strong and remember that Jeannie is watching over you." Then she put her arms around me and cried.

From that moment on, I was determined to make it through high school. I knew I'd always have to work harder than other students, but I also knew I could succeed.

And I truly believed that, if I needed strength, Jeannie would be there.

CHAPTER 15

Whenever Nita talked about junior high school, she talked about the dances; and whenever she talked about the dances, I'd have intimate thoughts about boys. She always made the dances sound very glamorous, so for me her stories sparked dreams of meeting guys, romantic evenings and staying out late.

In the fall of 1971, not long after I began junior high school, my parents allowed me to go to my first dance.

I remember burying myself amongst a large crowd outside the gym as we waited to get in. I did my best to be inconspicuous, but before long a familiar face was making its way towards me.

"Hi, Nova! How the hell are ya'?"

The voice was familiar, too. Then I realized it was Wayne, but he looked so different. He was wearing a spotless t-shirt with no obscene language and a fashionable pair of jeans; his hair was neatly combed and his smiling teeth seemed whiter than white.

"I bet you're waiting for that Penny chick you're always hanging around with," he went on.

"She-should-be … here … pret-ty-soon. Where's-the-rest-of … your-gang? Are-they-afraid-to … stay-out-late?"

"Ah, none of them have any money. I got the old lady to give me a few extra bucks. I think she'd rather have me here than on the streets." He said this with a snicker.

Without thinking about the vow I had made to myself regarding Wayne, I followed him over to some steps. Some people were already occupying them, but he made everyone move so we could sit down.

Soon it was like old times as we sat there talking about what the band might be like and how many people might show up.

Finally Penny arrived and found me, and like Wayne she was dressed to the hilt. She wore neatly pressed jeans and a light blue blouse, and her hair hung in pretty little ringlets.

All of a sudden I felt like a frump that had just crawled out from under a garbage can, so I tried to direct attention away from my wrinkled jeans and blouse and scuffed shoes by saying, "Penny ... this-is-Wayne ... an-old-friend."

Wayne seemed to stick to us like glue from then on. When we were inside and sitting in the gym bleachers, he made jokes about people around us and told stories about himself as a little kid. He even reminisced about the days when he and I had been good buddies and he'd taught me to inhale.

As soon as the band started to play, people began filling the dance floor. I was surprised when about half of them didn't dance; instead, they sat down cross-legged as close to the stage as possible, closed their eyes and swayed to the music. It looked to me like they were falling asleep rather than enjoying the music.

Then, to my surprise, Wayne asked me to dance. I was flattered because I'd always felt he was too good for me. *But why me and not Penny?* I wondered.

I felt shy at first because I had never danced amongst so many people. I loved dancing, but outside of a few sock hops in elementary school and dancing solo to the radio at home I had little experience.

Wayne knew what was going through my mind. He grabbed my hand and led me to the middle of the dance floor, saying, "Don't worry about it, Nova. Nobody's going to pay any attention to you. They're all getting into the band."

Wayne and I stayed out on the dance floor for quite a while. "You're a pretty good dancer!" he said at one point. But he also told me I watched my feet too much.

After three or four songs, he asked Penny to dance. He ended up dancing with her a lot longer. But I wasn't surprised; it made sense that he'd prefer to dance with a girl whose feet did what they were supposed to.

At about half past ten, Wayne and Penny accompanied me outside for a smoke. Then they walked me to a pay phone nearby where I called my Dad. I had to be home by eleven.

We chewed the fat until Dad arrived. As he drove up, they said a quick "Good night!" and scurried back to the dance.

During the next few weeks, Wayne was as friendly as could be, especially when Penny was around. But I knew what was going on. He and Penny were interested in being more than friends. And sure enough, romance blossomed for them. But as it did, first curiosity then jealousy blossomed for me. I knew it was crazy, but the friendlier they became the more jealous I felt.

At times I felt angry and left out whenever Penny and Wayne got close. But at other times I got vicarious pleasure out of their romance. And, because Penny would often meet up with Wayne at my house, I became part of his gang once again, which made me feel pretty important.

Whenever Wayne would put his arm around Penny, I'd feel

a spark of excitement go through me. I still felt jealous but also pleased that Wayne's girlfriend was my best friend.

The first time I saw them kissing one another, I wanted to run away because I felt so out of place. But I also wanted to watch because I was fifteen and very curious about sex. I hadn't necked with anyone since Jackie in the third grade, but I had a good idea what it was like. So secretly I wished I was in Penny's place.

Only once did Penny and I ever talk about my handicap, and as we chatted I shared my anxiousness about boys. "I'm-afraid … I'll-never-have … a-steady boyfriend," I remember saying to her. "My-CP … will-scare-them … away."

"Just be patient, Nova. If you let someone special get to know you and understand you, I'm sure that person will like you."

I hoped she was right.

⁓◌ℒ ℒ◌⁓

Mom gave me regular pep talks about what I could expect in my junior high school years. These times had been difficult for Flo and Jeannie, and because of my disabilities I was likely to have even more problems than they did.

A few times Mom brought up the issue of drugs. I remember her once saying with love, "High school is when kids get into that kind of thing, and you know, Nova, your brain is already damaged. That stuff could damage you even more, so please promise me you'll never go near it."

I then truthfully told her that I'd never touched dope of any kind and promised that until the day I died I'd never try it.

I was alarmed every time she mentioned the subject though because a few friends had recently started smoking marijuana. Wayne, for one, was into it pretty heavily. Penny and I had refused to try it, and I was proud of that. Still, I prayed my mother would never find out that some of my friends were involved.

I felt pretty relaxed about grade eight schoolwork that first year of junior high. But there were also some challenges to overcome.

For example, my Math teacher made no allowances for the difficulties my typewriter created. Furthermore, she was extremely conservative and strict; if your work wasn't up to standard, she assumed you were simply not paying attention. So because she wouldn't bend the rules or put in a little extra time with me, Math soon became my worst subject.

I tried to take French, but that turned out to be a fiasco. No matter how hard I struggled with the words, I couldn't pronounce them. Every time I tried, the class would erupt with laughter. After receiving an 'F' on my first report card, my French teacher recommended I take a study period instead.

Foods classes were also disastrous. Although I kept my notebook up to date and did the written assignments neatly, I was no good at cooking. Working with others in a cooking group was fun, but I couldn't pour a cup of milk or measure a teaspoon of salt. My spastic hands would not cooperate.

Nevertheless, because it was compulsory, I ended up staying in Foods. I participated in discussions and did written work, but I avoided the practical side as much as possible. I helped when I could, with simple tasks like scrubbing pans, but that was it.

My group's first creation was a batch of muffins, and I can remember agonizing over sitting down with the others to eat. To avoid embarrassment, I desperately tried to think of some way to get out of eating in front of them.

But one of the girls at the table seemed to read my mind. She buttered a muffin, handed it to me and said, "You helped. Go ahead and eat it. Anybody who doesn't want to watch can leave!"

I wasn't too fond of P.E. classes either. Our teacher, Mrs. Kadin, was a real slave driver. She was only five feet tall, but she had an extraordinary air of authority. Even the laziest people in the class moved when she shouted, "Move!"

One of her most grueling routines combined the Canadian Fitness Test exercises with a two-mile jog. After an hour of sit-ups, knee bends and the rest of the routine, I can remember feeling as though my body had been run over by a bulldozer.

But at least she made allowances for my condition. She expected me to try, but she never forced me into or through exercises I couldn't manage.

Still, sometimes Mrs. Kadin gave me heck for not putting in enough effort. It may sound odd, but I didn't mind. Some teachers would ignore me or make no demands because of my CP, but I'd be disappointed whenever this happened because being passed over made me feel more disabled than ever.

Mrs. Kadin caught on early to all of my tricks. She knew I'd sometimes use my handicap to get attention or to take it easy. But she wouldn't let me get away with a thing. I liked that.

ஒ௨ ௨௭

CHAPTER 16

ஒ௬ ௬௭

I n January, Mrs. Kadin announced that we'd be going skiing twice a week for two months.

"There's no problem if you're uncomfortable with downhill skiing," she said, looking at me. "There'll be snowshoeing through the back trails for non-skiers."

I decided right away that I had to try skiing. Furthermore, I made up my mind that no matter what happened, I wouldn't give up until I could ski the whole mile-long run down Kimberley's North Star Mountain.

Before I could learn to ski, I had to convince my mother I could survive.

"You have trouble walking, Nova," she argued. "How do you expect to ski? If you break your legs or, even worse, your back, you could spend the rest of your life in a wheelchair after all. I just can't let you take such a risk."

To hear the way Mom carried on, you'd think I was her only child heading off to war. *Come on, I'm almost sixteen years old!* I thought, frustrated.

Fortunately my father was more optimistic. "I think learning to ski is a great idea," he said. "And if you can do it, I'll even buy you your own ski equipment."

The two of them argued about it for quite awhile, but my Dad ended up winning.

He said, "Nova, you know better than anyone else what you can and can't do. And you've obviously made up your mind about this, so go ahead and give it a shot."

I remember my mother saying, "Fine, but if you break your neck, don't come to me for sympathy. I've taken care of you just about long enough, and I refuse to do it for the rest of my life."

I resented these words, but I kept quiet because I wanted to avoid a fight. *If I get into an argument with her, she might change her mind*, I thought.

Penny had Mrs. Kadin for P.E., too. And as our class boarded the bus for our first ski trip, I remember feeling thankful that my best friend had come along. If I needed moral support or a helping hand, I knew I could count on Penny.

Still, once we arrived at the rental shop everything was an ordeal, even with Penny's help. My first challenge was being fitted with equipment. After some searching, I located a pair of ski boots I could squeeze my feet into. However, I soon discovered I couldn't fasten the buckles. Even using all my strength, I couldn't snap them shut. I pushed so hard at one point that I toppled over in a somersault. Penny had to come to my rescue.

Next, we had to walk up a ramp onto a fitting platform to be equipped with skis, but walking in heavy ski boots was almost impossible. It took two men to help me up the ramp, and even then I had trouble keeping my balance. And worse, as I tried to lift my left foot into the ski binding, my leg went into a spasm and I nearly crushed the fingers of the man fitting me.

Once we'd been fitted with poles, Penny and I hurried out of the shop and looked for a place where we could put on our skis without anyone noticing. Neither of us had the slightest idea what we were doing. I did manage to get one ski on but then lost my footing and fell over backwards.

Fortunately Mrs. Kadin came along at that moment to help us. "You're off to a great start, Nova!" she laughed when she saw me lying there pinned in snow. "Now come on. Watch me."

She showed us how to clean the snow off the bottom of our boots, then place one boot in the binding and press hard to make everything snap into place. She stuck one ski pole in the snow, leaned on it to keep her balance and cleaned her boot with the other pole.

Penny followed her instructions and managed to get her skis on without any problems. But I had a lot of trouble placing my pole properly, not to mention keeping my balance long enough to grab the other pole and clean my boot with it. As soon as I lifted one foot off the ground, I landed flat on my back again.

Finally Mrs. Kadin gave up. As I lay there she lifted my leg, cleaned the soles of my boots and got me up and into my skis.

Pointing to the rest of our group, she said, "Off you go, now. And hurry! The first lesson is about to start."

The group gathered for lessons wasn't far away, so Mrs. Kadin got between us and helped us slide our way there. It was a struggle but we somehow managed to go the distance without a fall.

During the next few weeks, I made some progress. I learned how to get on and off the rope tow and even made a start coming down the 'bunny hill,' a short run reserved for youngsters and beginners. But I was hopeless at turning, and I couldn't stop myself once I got started.

Our instructor was very good looking. He had curly dark brown hair, a deep tan and eyes like two black diamonds. He looked as though he'd stepped out of the pages of a ski magazine. It didn't take long before I developed a mad crush on him.

At first he was friendly and asked me all kinds of questions like: "How many brothers or sisters do you have?" and "What do you do for excitement?" and "Where do you live?" I practically convinced myself he was in love with me.

I knew I didn't have much hope. I had realized long beforehand that guys weren't interested in girls like me. I had several crushes, but they always ended with the boy taking out another girl.

Even worse, sometimes they told me to my face, "You've got to be kidding!"

I feared that all my dreams of romance would remain just that – merely dreams.

When I mentioned the subject to Penny, she tried to reassure me: "There's someone for everyone in this world, Nova; someday you'll find the one for you. I think you're pretty."

Once Penny told me that an older man might be more understanding, and this got my hopes up concerning my ski instructor. I figured he must have been in his early twenties.

I soon found out, however, I wasn't the girl for him. As the lessons went on, he became less and less talkative. And at one point during our final lesson, he said, "Maybe you should take up snowshoeing instead."

But I was determined to ski. When I started down the hill on skis, a tremendous excitement surged through my body. It was the same feeling I had galloping down the hill near my house. When I fell the excitement vanished, but while it lasted it was wonderful! I was convinced that skiing was the sport for me.

When I told Mrs. Kadin that my ski instructor had pretty much decided I was useless on a pair of skis, she shook her head sadly. But she didn't agree that I should give up.

"We still have quite a few sessions left," she said. "I'm going to concentrate on helping you. I'm sure your classmates won't mind."

After school one day, I shared my frustrations with Mom over a cup of hot chocolate. But unlike Mrs. Kadin, she once again tried to discourage me. She was still afraid I'd injure myself permanently.

"All you need to do is break your back," she said. "You'd be worse off than the average person, Nova. I couldn't bear to see you with a more difficult handicap than you already have."

"But-Mom," I urged, "I-know ... that-in-time ... I'll-be-able ... to ski as-well-as ... the-next-person. Remem-ber what ... Dr.-Lang-said? He told me-to ... go-ahead-and-do ... anything-I-think I can-handle. As-for-falling, like I-told-Penny, it's-impos-sible ... for-me-to break-anything be-cause ... I'm-used-to ... falling. Most-people ... break-bones because ... they-stiffen-up ... when-they fall. But I-don't; I-just let-myself ... go."

Mom answered me with a look of loving concern, no more.

My ski instructor had given up on me, but Mrs. Kadin certainly hadn't.

"We'll show everyone that you can do it," I can remember her saying on the bus to North Star. "You'll see!"

She spoke with such confidence that I became more determined than ever to learn to ski. I didn't want to disappoint her.

Mrs. Kadin was a great ski instructor. First she showed me the proper way to stand still until I was ready to head downhill. Then she skied a quarter of the way down the bunny hill, looked back and signaled for me to follow her Z-shaped trail.

I started downhill shakily. I was able to make a left turn; however, on the right turn, my left limbs wouldn't cooperate and I fell face down.

After several more falls, Mrs. Kadin pinpointed my problem: "Your left leg isn't bending and turning. If you can lift your left leg and turn it in the air, you'll do much better. Watch."

She demonstrated, and I followed. With my skis plowing snow I made the left turn. I then concentrated on lifting my right ski off the snow, and as I lifted it I seemed to turn right automatically. There was almost no effort involved. I completed the turn and came to a stop beside Mrs. Kadin.

"That was terrific, Nova! Now, keep practicing on the bunny hill, and next week we'll try it from the top of the mountain."

At that moment I felt as though I had conquered the world.

Pretty soon the time came to try skiing the big run.

But first I had to get up the mountain, and riding the 'T-bar' was a failure. You don't sit on the T-bar lift. In a standing position, you let your bottom and whole body lean back as it pulls you and your partner up the hill.

I couldn't keep my balance in the leaning back position. Even though Mrs. Kadin coached and encouraged me, I'd always fall off a short distance up the mountain and wait dejectedly in a snowbank for her return.

"Maybe ... I-should-give-up," I said to her later as she helped me to my feet. "Maybe ... my-body's-not ... made-for-riding ... the-T-bar."

"This is no time for self-pity," she replied. "Now that you know how to ski downhill, all we have to do is get you to the top. Let me carry your poles. Maybe freeing up a hand will help you balance. Now come on, let's keep trying."

After a few more tries, I finally got the hang of it and rode the T-bar to the top of the run. I did have another spill while dismounting, but Mrs. Kadin comforted me by telling me that all beginners had the same problem. "You'll push off like a pro next time," she said encouragingly.

Skiing down North Star Mountain my first time was like speeding down a big hill in roller skates. I fell many times, of course, but only because I was afraid of picking up too much speed. Luckily, the snow was a lot softer higher up the mountain, so falling didn't bother me.

Halfway down, however, we came to a halt at a steep stretch of bumps Mrs. Kadin called 'moguls.' The name sounded menacing and I didn't like the look of them.

Before this part of the hill, Mrs. Kadin had been skiing in front of me, stopping regularly to let me catch up. But when we hit the moguls, she said, "You go first. That way, if anything goes wrong, I can ski down to where you are and help you."

After a close look, I figured the easiest way through them would be to ski a wide zigzagging course. I started off as slowly as possible, but as I went over and through the big bumps, I picked up way too much speed. I was forced to make myself fall, but this time I couldn't stop. All the way to the bottom of the moguls my body kept spinning and bumping and rolling.

Not long after I came to a halt, I gazed up to see Mrs. Kadin looking down on me with an odd expression. She seemed concerned, but she was also smiling. I think she'd had a good laugh.

I loved skiing at North Star Mountain. Going down the hill I felt so free. I imagined I was Nancy Greene!

Mrs. Kadin gave me several more lessons, and before long my skiing was so good that she felt comfortable leaving me on my own.

By the time the ski season was over, the mile-long run at North Star, including the moguls, took me fifteen minutes.

My father was so pleased with my progress that he kept his promise and bought me skis, boots and poles at a spring sale. It was too warm to use my new equipment, but winter was never far away in Kimberley.

I loved seeing the shock on people's faces when I told them I skied, and I could hardly wait for the next ski season. I was sure that by the end of it I'd be taking on North Star like a pro.

CHAPTER 17

ఆఠ ఆఠ

As I entered the final months of the eighth grade, things seemed to be going along smoothly – that is, until the morning a psychologist named Dr. Davis visited Mrs. Kadin's Guidance class.

He spoke to us about mental retardation, which I found interesting but a little too close to home. His talk brought back memories of being at Pinewood, where most of my classmates and friends were retarded. Even though I knew I could think normally and that I wasn't mentally retarded, it didn't take long until I began feeling as though he was talking about me.

"Retarded children are easy to recognize. Many have spastic coordination and talk in a slow and awkward way." The man who said these words had a bald spot on the top of his head and long hair around the sides; he wore a plaid shirt, faded blue jeans and old hiking boots. He certainly didn't look like any professional I'd ever seen.

Still, as our hippy-like visitor spoke I began to wonder about myself, and toward the end of his presentation I found myself squeezing back tears.

Since I had been taken out of Pinewood, the only time my

handicap bothered me was when I was teased or just feeling sorry for myself. Why this so-called doctor got to me, I didn't know.

The bell rang to end the period, and as soon as we were dismissed I dashed out of class. As I entered the hallway I could feel the tears rolling.

From behind I could hear Penny call out, "Nova, wait!"

Ignoring her, I rushed off. As I pushed through the crowded hallway, it felt as though everyone was watching me. I didn't know where I was going, but I dared not stop.

Suddenly, someone grabbed my arm and pulled me out of the noisy hallway into a quiet lobby. It was the Girls' Counselor. "Come into my office, Nova," she said, trying to be tender. "Tell me what's bothering you. Maybe I can help."

In her office I just couldn't come out with what I felt inside. I had spoken to this woman before and didn't feel comfortable with her, so I stalled.

"Noth-ing's-the … mat-ter," I insisted over and over.

I'm not sure she was convinced, but after many minutes she finally let me go.

I was surprised to find Penny waiting for me in the lobby. Two other classmates, Nancy and Tracy, were with her.

As they led me back into the hallway, Tracy said, "Nova, are you all right? I watched you all through Dr. Davis' talk. You shouldn't feel he was talking about you." This was the first time Tracy had ever seemed interested in my handicap.

"Besides," continued Penny, "almost everyone in this school knows you're as mentally with it as the next person." Penny's voice was comforting, without pity.

Then Nancy said, "Don't forget, Nova, you're not the only one with a speech problem. I have one, too, but there isn't anybody who's going to tell me I'm mentally retarded." I liked Nancy; she had a way of making advice funny, yet sensible.

I was thankful to all three of them for caring so much, but I began to feel stupid for the way I had behaved.

Of course the psychologist wasn't referring to me, I thought. *He probably didn't even know that there was something abnormal about me as I sat in the classroom. He probably didn't notice me at all.*

My last class before lunch that day was P.E., and just before it started Mrs. Kadin spoke to me. "Now Nova, I'll bet you know what this is going to be about," she began as she reached down to tie her running shoes.

For sure I thought she was going to bawl me out.

"I watched your reaction during the Guidance class today," she went on. "I can understand to a certain degree why you related your situation to what Dr. Davis was saying. But, at the same time, you should feel lucky you are what you are, and grateful you're not like the people he was referring to."

The way she talked I knew she was being reasonable.

Still, I tried to explain: "But ... I-noticed ... some-of-the-girls ... turning-their-heads ... towards-me, like-they ... were-thinking ... he-was ... talking-about ... me."

"That's silly. Some of the students and staff don't understand your CP, but the majority of people who've had any contact with you know there's nothing wrong with your brain – at least nothing worse than anybody else's." She smiled and added, "Now, to set your mind at ease, I've asked Dr. Davis to speak to you this afternoon. I'll arrange for you to be excused from your final class. I'm sure it won't be the first class you've missed for a good reason." Then she winked.

I had mixed feelings about an appointment with Dr. Davis. I felt embarrassed about the way I had behaved. He likely had no idea a handicapped person was in the classroom. I also hoped that since he was a psychologist he could help sort out my feelings.

Over lunch Penny said, "Don't be nervous. If the conversation doesn't work out and you feel foolish, keep in mind that you'll probably never see the guy again."

My appointment with Dr. Davis was in the classroom used for Guidance classes. I was surprised when Penny met me at the back door; she had somehow gotten the permission to join me. Still, we remained silent as we walked in.

Dr. Davis wasn't there yet, so we claimed two desks at the front of the classroom. But before we could have a few words, Dr. Davis entered through the front door. "Hello, sorry I'm a bit late," he said, settling into the wooden chair usually occupied by Mrs. Kadin.

After a few moments, he looked at me and asked, "Are you Nova?" Then he turned to Penny with a blank look.

"I'm Penny," she said. "Nova asked me to come. I'm sort of … kind of … a supporter, you might say. I hope you don't mind." Penny gave him a friendly look, a look that said if he did mind she'd be disappointed.

"Oh no," the doctor answered. "I understand. Now Nova, I've been told about your reaction to my talk this morning. I want to first say that I'm very sorry for upsetting you. I can't say I didn't see you there, but I was unaware of your disability. To me you looked like an average girl in a grade eight class."

I took this as a compliment.

He went on to say, "Anybody in your situation would have felt the same way."

"What-got ... to-me ... was-when-you ... said-that ... the-way-to-tell ... re-tard-a-tion ... was-by-poor-speech ... and-lack-of ... co-ord-in-a-tion," I replied.

"No, if I said it that way, I didn't mean it to sound that way. First of all, not all retarded people are like that. Second, while CP and mental retardation sometimes seem close together, the two conditions are far apart."

After fifteen minutes had gone by, I felt a hundred percent better; and as he continued talking, he told us about many people with CP he'd met. "I know one fellow, more spastic than you, who just graduated from university with a degree in Journalism. He's confined to a wheelchair, so it may not be easy for him to find a job with a newspaper, but he's full of determination."

Dr. Davis gave other similar examples, and the more he talked about different kinds of physical and mental handicaps, the more I wanted to know.

As we talked I found out a lot about careers, too. I even found out what to take in high school, college and university to become a rehabilitation counselor.

We talked right up until the bell sounded. I could have stayed there for hours, but I didn't want to keep him.

"Thanks-for ... your-time," I said with honesty.

"Yes, thanks," said Penny.

As all three of us left the classroom, I realized I had learned a valuable lesson: instead of worrying about what others were saying or thinking, I needed to concentrate more on my future. *Maybe one day, if I work hard, I'll be counseling a disabled person who's been hurt by taking something the wrong way*, I thought.

I later mentioned my dream of becoming a rehabilitation

counselor to our Girls' Counselor, but she was less encouraging than Dr. Davis. "Judging from your grades in Math, Nova, and the fact that you've dropped French, you'd better stick to the vocational program," she said.

"Don't listen to her," said Penny on our way home. "A lot can change by the time you get to senior high school."

By the end of grade eight, Penny had become my best friend. She was understanding enough to relate to me without pity and stubborn enough to stand up to me whenever I got difficult.

We had several talks about what it was like for me to have CP. She asked curious things: "How does it feel when people are scared of you?" or "What's it like when you face strangers?"

Outside of members of my family, Penny was the only person since Jeannie who really understood me. Furthermore, she could predict when I'd have trouble managing something and she'd step in to help. If she knew I could manage by myself she'd make me try.

Best of all, not only would she stick up for me if I got teased, but she'd try to help my tormentors understand my handicap. Anytime kids asked why I was different, she'd explain completely – as expertly as any member of my family.

Still, Penny and I did have the occasional fight.

One time, on our way to the arena, we got cocky and started putting down one another's parents. It got so bad we started slapping each other, and before long we were on the ground trying to scratch each other's eyes out.

We didn't quit scrapping until Penny's sisters, walking not far behind, pulled us apart. I was kind of glad about that because Penny had me pinned down and was getting the best of me.

The crazy things Penny and I did and the crazy situations we found ourselves in more than made up for our few disagreements.

In Social Studies class one day I pulled a cough drop out of my pocket, intending to pop it into my mouth. But my hand gave a little jerk and it ended up dropping down my blouse and into my bra. It landed in a very uncomfortable spot; I knew that trying to get it out without anyone noticing was going to be impossible.

Nevertheless, I snuck my hand under the bottom of my blouse and then up until I could feel my bra. I wanted to stretch it out, with the hope that the cough drop would fall out. Knowing my typewriter case was hiding me from the teacher and most of my classmates, I tugged and tugged on my bra.

Penny sat right across from me and saw. To her it must have seemed as though I was fooling around under my top. I couldn't let Penny think I was playing with myself so I pulled out my hand and mouthed "*cough drop!*" trying to get her to read my lips.

As soon as she understood, she let out a split second shriek of laughter, just enough to interrupt the class. With that everyone was staring our way. Soon Penny and I were paralyzed with teary-eyed giggling.

But our teacher, Mr. Spect, was fuming. "Penny and Nova, you can both remain after the bell and explain what's so funny!" He sounded so serious he was able to scare our giggles away, and we sat there worrying for the rest of the class.

How embarrassing, I thought. *How will I explain this?*

Penny must have read my mind. At one point she glanced at me and shook her head, as if to say that she'd never give in and tell.

Penny kept her word. In the empty classroom with Mr. Spect

asking us over and over what we were laughing about, "Nothing" was our answer.

Finally he gave up and let us go with a warning: "If you ever interrupt my class again, I swear I'll paddle both of your behinds with this ruler!"

Penny and I must have known he meant business because we somehow held our laughter until we made it to the girls' washroom, where we extracted the cough drop.

CHAPTER 18

T he summer before grade nine my parents must have needed a break from me because as soon as the holidays began they suggested I head to Lethbridge to help Nita look after my nephews.

Nita had actually been living with Flo and Stewart since early spring. She seemed happier in Lethbridge when we had visited occasionally on weekends – maybe because she had developed a pretty serious relationship with a boy named Jerry.

I didn't blame Nita for wanting to move away. She had battled with my parents for years. They were critical of her friends and just about everything she did; if she tried to date someone or get the most out of a party at the lake, they did their best to make things difficult for her.

Nita had a few problems living with our older sister, too. For one thing, Flo felt she was spending too much time with Jerry. Nita, on the other hand, was always complaining about Flo's rules.

I couldn't see how she had any right to complain. She got free room and board, money whenever she babysat Stewart Jr.,

Johnny, and Chris, and dating privileges away from Mom and Dad. To me, Nita was lucky.

Even though Flo and Stewart were fairly strict with Nita and me, summer babysitting for them certainly had its good points. We could have a smoke once the boys were in bed and stay up as late as we wanted. I missed Penny, but other than that it was a nice change from spending the whole summer in Kimberley.

However, I didn't feel too secure walking around in Lethbridge. Even walking down to the corner store was a challenge. It seemed like as soon as anybody new saw me I'd be mocked and belittled. Once I was even beaten up.

Another time a cop in a paddy wagon stopped me and asked my name, where I lived, and where I was going. When I gave answers, he looked at me in that suspicious way that said he was judging me by my looks, not my brains. He let me go, but followed me all the way back home.

In that Alberta town, it seemed the only safe place was inside Flo and Stewart's house. And yet, even there I often felt nervous. When they'd have company, or Stewart Jr. brought one of his little friends home, or Nita invited Jerry over, I'd do my best to make myself scarce. In front of new people, I was still very embarrassed about my shaking and speaking.

When I left Lethbridge that summer I felt a little sad, because I knew Nita was staying for good. It looked like there would be no reconciliation with my parents. From then on, it was going to be just Mom, Dad and me living in Kimberley.

✿ ✿

One Sunday afternoon in mid-September 1972, as I arrived home from doing homework at Penny's, I saw a car with Alberta plates pull into our driveway. I knew it wasn't Stewart and Flo, because they had a beaten-up black Volkswagen. This was a pretty hot car, a souped-up red Firebird.

As I walked up behind the car, four people got out. The first two I didn't recognize, but the two who climbed out of the back seat were Jerry and Nita.

When I saw my sister and her boyfriend, excitement surged through me and I rushed to greet them. They each gave me a kiss and hug and introduced me to their friends, Tina and Rick.

As I nodded my head to Nita and Jerry's friends, embarrassment took over. I got visions of what I must have looked like running towards them with spastic legs. For sure, they must have thought I was mentally retarded.

That worry left me when I noticed Mom and Dad coming out of the house. They weren't sharing my excitement at Nita coming home. In fact, they both seemed displeased. Right then and there I realized I didn't have the slightest idea what was going on.

I got the feeling, though, that Mom and Dad knew about Nita's visit beforehand and were keeping something from me. Something was wrong. I wanted to know what.

Unfortunately, my curiosity had to wait because my parents asked me to go back to Penny's for a few hours while they had a visit with Nita and Jerry.

Penny and I were sitting on the curb in front of her house sharing one of her mother's cigarette butts and speculating about what was going on when the Firebird pulled up beside us.

I got up quickly and went straight to the open back window where I knew Nita and Jerry would be sitting. When I looked in I noticed that Nita's eyes were all red and watery: something really was wrong. Nita could turn on the tears in a second to get what she wanted from my parents, but this wasn't anywhere near like that.

"Nova, Jerry and I are getting married. That's why we came here, to tell Mom and Dad our plans." Nita said these words with a shiver in her voice.

I guess I must have had a "you've got to be joking" look on my face because Jerry took Nita's left hand and held it up to my face. On her finger was a small diamond ring.

For the second time that day I felt surges of excitement running through me! "When?" I asked.

"December, we don't know exactly, but you'll be coming to Lethbridge with Mom and Dad for the wedding." Nita's sadness seemed to be disappearing.

Then Jerry spoke. "We were supposed to tell you to go home for dinner. Your Mom was putting everything on when we left." He used his usual bossy tone of voice. "And you'd better go right now or we'll drive back and tell on you for smoking," he kidded.

"Aren't-you-guys … staying-for … supper?" I asked.

"No, Rick has to work tomorrow and so do I," Jerry explained. "See you in a few weeks! Your parents are coming to help us get things ready."

As they drove off, a thousand-and-one questions ran through my head: *How could they get married? Had they even been going steady for a year? Why would they drive all the way from Lethbridge? Why not wait until we visited them next? Wasn't December a little too soon to pull off a wedding?*

But then more positive questions came to my mind: *Would I be in the wedding party? Or, would Nita be too embarrassed to have me? If I was in the wedding party, would I be matron of honour? Or, would Nita have a simpler wedding because it was so soon?*

I said good-bye to Penny and rushed home to see if I could get some answers.

When I entered the house, Mom was in her chair watching television. She had a dishtowel over her shoulder, which indicated it was mealtime. Like Nita, her nose was red and her eyes were watery.

Dad was asleep on the couch, so she quietly said, "Sit down, dear. I have something to tell you. Did you see your sister?"

"Ya ... they-told-me-to ... come-home-for ... dinner ... and-then-we ... said-good-bye. What's-wrong?" I asked, not saying anything about a wedding.

"Nita's getting married next month. We have to go to Lethbridge soon to make arrangements. There's little time." I knew by the tone of Mom's voice that there was something else, and the excited feeling surged through me again.

"You have to know this, I guess," she said. "Nita's pregnant. We're not ashamed of her or anything, but it's come as a shock to your Dad and me."

I was so surprised for a few moments that I didn't know how to react or what to say. "Are-you-happy ... about-it?" I couldn't tell if this question was only in my mind or whether the words came out.

Mom soon answered. "We love your sister just like we love you. I think she's a little young, but if she wants to get married and have a baby I guess we'll have to go along with it. They both love each other, they say, and Jerry seems to be a nice boy. Your father told Jerry he'd have to cut his hair, but otherwise we'll bless them." As she said these words, she sounded a little happier.

⁖⊕⊕ ⊕⊕⁖

The wedding was set for the fifth of December, and we ended up traveling to Lethbridge a couple of weeks after Nita and Jerry's visit.

As we drove there, all my parents could talk about was how much we had to do, in so little time.

I ended up spending most of the weekend babysitting for Flo and Stewart while they helped with the wedding preparations. Without Nita around to help, I had my hands full looking after my three nephews!

My sister and brother-in-law were out so late Saturday evening that I had to get the boys ready for bed on my own.

They usually had a snack before bed, but there was no way I was going to prepare their favourite, popcorn. It would just end up half-popped all over the floor. Thank goodness they agreed to have cookies instead.

Stewart Jr., who was seven, was old enough by then to understand why I couldn't handle most of the choices their mother or Nita offered. He even took care of pouring milk for himself and his brothers, knowing that with Auntie Nova there was a chance that the milk would spill.

I couldn't get the boys to go to bed that night until they saw my temper. I lost control and yelled loud enough to wake the whole neighbourhood. Finally, I got so mad that I belted little five-year-old Chris in the shoulder, knocking him to the floor.

He cried loudly for so long I was afraid I'd broken something in his little body. I talked to him gently for a long time and luckily got him to trust me again. I cuddled him to sleep and ended up falling asleep myself, amongst all three boys in Flo and Stewart's big bed.

In the morning, I worried that the boys would complain about how mean I had been, but they acted like nothing happened. I felt lucky and promised myself I'd never hit one of them again.

For the next two weeks – at school, our home or my friends' houses – all I could talk about was Nita's wedding.

Even though I secretly hoped to be in Nita's wedding party, the prospect scared me to death. I had visions of walking wobbly down the aisle, my bouquet falling apart before I reached the altar. And I knew I'd get that embarrassed feeling that everyone was looking at my spastic way of walking.

As it turned out, all my worrying was for nothing. Nita chose Doreen, a high school friend, to be her matron of honour and decided not to have any other bridesmaids.

I felt a mixture of emotions over Nita's decision. I was relieved, but I was also hurt at being left out. I was jealous. Nita would be the centre of attention. This was what I had always endured growing up with her. She was the better one because she was 'normal.'

Mom knew exactly how I felt and tried to calm the waters: "Nita's wedding isn't going to be a large one. Therefore, there's only one bridesmaid, and that's Doreen. She didn't exclude you because you have CP, or for any other reason. She and Doreen have been good friends for years, and you know that. If you were in Nita's place, you'd probably be choosing Penny, right?"

Mom made a lot of sense, so even though it was hard, I accepted Nita's decision.

The day of the wedding, the bride and the rest of our family got ready at Flo and Stewart's place.

When I went into the master bedroom to attempt to dress myself, Mom was in her slip attending to Nita. My sister's beautiful

Nita and Jerry so happy at their wedding. As was typical in our small town, the bride and groom were teenagers.

wedding gown was already on. As I fumbled into my panty hose and dress, I watched Mom arranging Nita's long white veil and wavy hair, which both reached the middle of her back.

I had just finished dressing when my father came in to take Nita to the church. The ceremony went rather well, but the huge chapel of the church was barely one third full. Only members of our family and Jerry's family and a few friends that the couple knew in Lethbridge were there.

I sat beside Johnny, Stewart's brother who was seventeen,

only a year older than me. It looked like he was my escort, which made me feel more a part of things, and less of an outcast.

Soon after Jerry and Nita were pronounced husband and wife, everyone followed them outside the church, exchanged hugs and wished them well.

The funniest part happened soon after Johnny and I followed Flo and Stewart into their car. We had intended to follow the wedding car all over town (speeding and beeping), but we lost it soon after it left.

The four of us decided to head back to Stewart and Flo's for a drink. As long as my parents were out of sight, they were out of mind, and I was treated like an adult. Not only did I have a cigarette, I sucked back a beer with the handy straw I always carried.

Eventually, our party of four made its way to the reception hall and found a seat. Everything was in full swing, so there were no questions asked.

During mealtime, Mom left the head table and came over to see what she could get for me. This embarrassed and disappointed me because Johnny understood my condition and would have given me all the help I needed. Instead of showing I was ungrateful, I asked my mother to bring me a couple of buns full of meat, as they'd be the easiest to eat.

After a short dinner the bar opened. I was sure my parents wouldn't mind me having a few drinks; after all, at sixteen years old, a beer or two was nothing new to me. But, as my luck always seemed to end up, I forgot my straw at Flo and Stewart's and the hall was out of them. There was no way I was going to ask anyone to pour booze down my throat, so I decided to go without.

Jerry, my new brother-in-law, must have gotten wind of my dilemma because he came over to me just before the band started up and said, "Nova, you have to have a sip of something to welcome me into the family."

He knew how embarrassed I got when someone fed me, especially in front of strangers, so he took me behind the piano for a sip of his screwdriver. No sooner did he get the glass away from my mouth than someone hit a piano key.

"Oh, oh, that's my cue – for the first dance!" he half-shouted, half-whispered in my ear.

He then gave me a quick kiss on the cheek, grabbed my hand and led me from behind the piano, to face many eyes that had begun searching for the groom.

Nita and some other people who saw us emerge must have wondered what was going on. But soon after, when Jerry took Nita into his arms to start the first dance, I saw him whispering in her ear. Then they both turned to smile at me.

Before the reception was over, I had quite a few more sips from Jerry's drinks, and embarrassment was the furthest thing from my mind.

I celebrated and danced with just about everyone long into the night.

༄༅ ༄༅

Nita gave birth to my fourth nephew, Gerald Wayne Jr., in April 1973. A niece named Jeannine and nicknamed "Jeannie" would be born almost exactly a year later.

CHAPTER 19

O ne of the great things about being in junior high school was getting out a week earlier than the elementary students, but that was only if you passed all your classes and didn't have to write final exams.

In grade nine Penny and I did well enough to finish early. We decided to go camping before reporting back on the last day to pick up our report cards.

We planned to make an abandoned campground at nearby Munro Lake our "home away from home" for almost a week.

Penny and I had great fun planning our camping trip (the equipment and clothes we would need, food and utensils, etc.).

Both sets of parents were okay with our plans because our friend Ruby, along with her mother and brothers, were going to be staying in a cabin not far from the campground. Tiny, Ruby's mom, promised to look out for us.

Dixie, Penny's shaggy grey-haired pooch, would be there to look out for us, too.

Penny's mom drove us to the campground and helped us unpack. We soon discovered that we'd forgotten to bring air mattresses, so as Mrs. Stanley drove off we rushed into the tent and practiced lying in our sleeping bags on the rock hard floor.

Close to dusk, Ruby and her older brother Bob dropped by to see how we were doing. Right away Bob took our food and hung it from a distant tree.

"You don't want bears in your camp in the middle of the night, do you?" he half-warned, half-teased.

"Bears? Are-there … a-lot … around-here?" I asked.

"Nova," Ruby said, as if she was a teacher and I was her pupil, "you're out in the sticks now. Of course there are bears. As a matter of fact, you're invading their territory."

"But, we've got Dixie," said Penny, and then a worried expression crossed her face. "Dixie? Dixie!"

After twenty minutes of searching for Penny's little dog, I excused myself to search for the outhouse. Before long it would be too dark to follow the trail. Getting to the outhouse through the undergrowth was a challenge, but after a little bush whacking I made it.

The square building looked like it had been there for as long as the lake. Just about all the paint had peeled off, and at first I was reluctant to go in. I was afraid that it might collapse, and I'd be trapped in an old-fashioned sewage plant.

As the door squeaked open on its poorly sprung hinges, it bumped into something that began scratching at the door. I felt my heart skipping beats as the beast came scrambling out.

It was Dixie, and she was shaking more than I was. Our guard dog had been found.

Bears, the cold hard ground – Penny and I couldn't sleep that first night, so we carried our sleeping bags and guard dog over to Ruby's cabin at the first crack of dawn, and we pleaded with

Tiny to let us stay. She was a good sport, and we ended up getting a little bit of sleep before breakfast.

Later that day, I was standing on the dock with Penny, Ruby and Tiny, and Ruby said, "Hey Nova, I think it's time you learned how swim!" and she pushed me into the water. I went in headfirst and began dogpaddling frantically within arms reach.

I wasn't in danger because I could dogpaddle in our city pool, but I started laughing and sucking in water. I remember Tiny yelling, "Don't swallow the whole lake!"

I dogpaddled back to the dock and the three of them pulled me out. They were laughing hysterically as I stood there shivering and giggling on the dock.

Finally, I sputtered, "Well … now-I … know … how-to-swim … in-a-lake!"

The second night we had some visitors almost as annoying as bears. Wayne (by this time Penny's former boyfriend) and some of his friends showed up drunk and crashed our campfire.

Luckily, I thought of a way to get rid of them. I reminded Wayne about the time he helped me up a slippery hill in the middle of winter. "Ya … you-had-your-Boy-Scout … uniform-on … remember?" I taunted. "I-guess-you-figured … instead-of-tease-me … you'd-do-your … good-deed … for-the-day."

Everyone around the fire broke into laughter.

"But, but …" he stammered with an embarrassed look on his face, "You lie! I've never been a Boy Scout."

Soon after that, he rounded up his buddies and took off.

I thought Penny, Ruby and I would make a pretty good three-some, but during the rest of our stay at Munro Lake there were times when the two of them talked among themselves or abandoned me.

A number of times they took off together in Tiny's motorboat without me. There was really no reason for not asking me along, and with each excursion I felt more and more left out.

I was ready to end my friendship with Penny by the time her mother arrived to bring us home.

On the last day of school I ran into Penny as we picked up our report cards, and she apologized.

"I'm sorry, Nova. I know Ruby and I kind of ignored you up at the lake." Her words proved she was a pretty sensitive person, even though she hadn't behaved that way.

"It's-okay … at-least … you-an'-Rube … got-to-know … each-other … bet-ter." Still feeling hurt but wanting our friend-ship to carry on, I added, "Hey-may-be.. you'd-like-to … help-me-baby-sit … this sum-mer … in-Leth-bridge."

Penny must have been as keen as I was to spend the summer vacation in a bigger city because she said, "That sounds fantas-tic! I'll ask Mom and Dad tonight."

After supper she called with good news. "I'm coming with you," she informed me and went on to say, "It's weird, they're almost happy to let me go."

Having Penny stay in Lethbridge was great.

For one thing, there was someone to talk to when Flo and Stewart were working nights and the boys were in bed.

For another thing, during the daytime I had some protection if the destination was downtown, the park or the swimming pool. And regularly we'd visit Nita to chuckle over soap operas or give her a break from little Gerald.

Near the end of our stay, Penny got friendly with Flo and Stewart's old paperboy, Roland.

I had known "Rolly," as Flo called him, for a couple of years, not that he paid much attention to me.

I thought he was weird because even in the summer he wore a black top hat and a long black coat accompanied by a striped scarf; and everywhere he went he carried a black cane. He must have been about six feet tall, and as he walked, his long fine auburn hair would dance wildly below his hat.

If he'd been seen in Kimberley, everyone would have thought he'd escaped from an insane asylum. I never thought a guy like that would attract Penny.

However, when I introduced them, they seemed to look deeply at each other. He asked Penny all sorts of questions, and the next day he gave her little hints that he cared for her, like getting after her for smoking.

Never had Rolly said more than a quick "Hi" or "Bye" to me. *Either he doesn't understand my speech or he's afraid that if we're seen on the street chatting he might be accused of socializing with a retard*, I thought once I realized Penny liked him back.

I remember asking Flo, "Do-you-think … Rol-ly-knows … my-handi-cap's … phys-i-cal … not-men-tal?"

"Of course, you're being silly," she said.

Maybe, I thought, *but he sure treats Penny differently*.

One night, Rolly dropped by to see Penny.

As we sat on the couch watching TV, the two of them started to wrestle around. I didn't know what to do – help Penny out like she asked me to every once in a while, ignore them and keep watching TV, or just go to bed.

Then the living room went completely silent, and out of the corner of my eye I could see them getting pretty intimate. I decided at that point to go to bed, and as I walked out of the room,

I glanced back to see them getting about as close as you can get with your clothes on.

I said, "G'-night," but the two of them never replied.

I was surprised when not long after I was settled in bed, I heard the front door slam shut, followed by footsteps.

I thought, *I wonder if I should go and see what happened? But then Penny will know I feel jealous and threatened, this time because Rolly's interfering in our friendship, not Ruby.*

It wasn't long before Penny came into the room we shared, flicked on the light and said, "Why did you take off on me?"

I knew her well enough to read the anger in her eyes. "I-wasn't … en-joy-ing … watch-ing-you-two … get-to-know … each-other … bet-ter," I snapped back, trying to match her tone of voice.

"Thanks to you he thought he could get a little bit off me. Luckily, he took *no* for an answer." She sounded truly relieved.

"Well … what-was-I … sup-posed-to-do … pull-him-away … give-him-a-lec-ture … on-how-he … should-behave … with-a-girl … he-met … two-days-ago?" I did my best not to yell and show my temper.

It didn't take long though before I started calling Penny names, and she returned the worst back to me.

We only stopped because Flo come in the front door, and we probably both went to sleep with the same thing in mind: *I'll never speak to her again!*

The next morning, after ignoring Penny for a while, I broke the ice by joking, "I-guess … Rolly-won't-be … rolling-around-here … any-more."

"The jerk," she said, which told me she had written the guy off and was ready to salvage our friendship.

We apologized for our behaviour the night before and vowed we'd never leave one another under those circumstances again.

We patched things up just in time, right before the Labour Day long weekend. Flo and Stewart had promised to treat us to a camp out at Wasa Lake before returning us to Kimberley, and we'd been looking forward to it.

I had woken up fearing Penny would want to go home. Instead, we excitedly prepared for our second camping trip together.

We arrived at Wasa Lake, which is close to Kimberley, late Friday afternoon. My sister and brother-in-law were professional campers compared to Penny and me, so we let them set up while we looked after the boys.

"Go ahead, you two!" said Flo, when they were done. She knew we were anxious to get to the beach for a swim.

Actually, it was the people we were most interested in. We wondered whether there would be anybody we knew from Kimberley, or any good-looking guys.

The first guy we ran into in the beach parking lot was far from good looking. He looked like a biker with long scraggly black hair and beard, dirty-looking t-shirt and jeans, tattoos down both arms, cigarette in one hand and a beer in the other. He was the sort of guy your mother warns you to stay away from.

Beside him was a friend, a guy who seemed the complete opposite. He had longish blond hair, neatly combed, and a face that looked like it would never need a razor. He had a great tan and wore nothing but faded cut-off jeans.

The thing that really intrigued me about this guy was that when we saw him later at the beach he sat away from everyone else, just playing a guitar.

In the evening when we went for a stroll, there he was again, strumming down by the water. I couldn't help but imagine that he was serenading me. I wanted to go right up to him and introduce myself, and make friends. But I just couldn't get up the nerve.

All he became was a topic of conversation between Penny and me, and another romantic fantasy.

Later in the evening, a few of Stewart's friends from Kimberley dropped by our campsite. Never before had I realized that my brother-in-law had such good-looking friends.

One of them, Mike, was like an actor in a movie or TV show. Like the troubadour on the beach, he had blond hair, blue eyes and a deep dark tan. He also had a mustache that matched his hair colour and a personality that matched his looks. He could get any girl he wanted.

At first Penny said he was conceited. But later, around the campfire, I noticed her getting pretty talkative with him. Just before it was time for bed, he asked her if she'd like to go for a drive around the lake.

I was surprised that my sister and brother-in-law let Penny go; after all, Mike was at least five years older than her.

But off they went, and I was left alone to get ready for bed.

There was no way I could sleep with Penny gone, so I got up and sat by the fire, glaring into the coals.

I was mad at the world. I was mad at Flo and Stewart for letting Penny go. I was mad at Penny because she hadn't taken me along for security reasons. I was also mad at being too handicapped for Mike. *If I wasn't so shaky and retarded looking, maybe he'd have taken me instead of Penny*, I thought.

I imagined myself sitting beside him in his red T-Bird, the radio blasting, him giving me all those looks that guys give girls when they're out on dates. I was so busy getting steamed up that I didn't notice Flo join me.

"What's the matter with you? You look like you're ready to kill," she said. "Penny's not back?" She sounded concerned.

"No," I answered. "I-have-no … i-dea … where-they-could've-gone. You-sup-pose … some-thing-could … have-hap-pened?" I wanted to sound worried enough that Flo might send Stewart looking for them.

"I'm sure they've gone for coffee somewhere, probably to get to know each other better. I'm going to sleep, and you should do the same. Night, Nova." She gave me a kiss on the cheek.

Eventually, when the fire died down, I did go to bed. Penny and I were to sleep in Flo and Stewart's most recent car, an enormous four-door Pontiac, with her in the front seat and me in the back. I tossed for half an hour before falling asleep.

A few hours later, I awoke when I heard Penny climbing into the front seat.

I give her credit for trying to be quiet, I thought. But as soon as the car door shut, I opened my eyes and my brain began to race.

It must have been at least five a.m., the sun just starting to rise behind the Rocky Mountains. I knew it was better for me to just pretend I was sleeping, but I had to say something.

"Where did you go?" I snarled her way.

"To the Husky station for coffee, then to the cabaret. We shut the place down, drove around the lake, and ended up necking on the beach." From the way Penny answered me I could tell she'd detected I was in a jealous mood. She said her part fast, like a smart-assed teenager giving her parent a run down on the evening's events.

"Did-you-get … asked-for … I.D.?"

"No, I guess because I was with Mike they took it for granted I was old enough. The waitress did give me a funny look, though, when I ordered a white rum and coke. I only had two all night. I can't tell you what the band was like, because we talked most of the time."

"Did-Mike … try-any-thing?" I knew this was none of my business, but I had to ask.

"Well, he brought a blanket along to the beach. I knew what he wanted, but he didn't get it. After we necked for a while, he brought me back. Nova, let's go to sleep."

I persisted. "Are-you-going … to-see-him … a-gain? Do-you … like-him? Do-you … think-be-cause … you-turned-him-down … he'll-think-you're … a-candy-ass?"

"Fuck off, Nova!"

Hearing that, I felt a terrible temper come over me and I leaped into the front seat. I found myself pulling and slapping at Penny, and she gave it back to me. But I was determined to win this fight, so I dug my nails into her scalp and then raked them down her face. That made her stop fighting and start wailing with pain.

My anger and jealousy vanished as I realized what I'd done to my best friend. I felt only fear, because Penny was hiding her face with her hands and blood was oozing between her fingers.

Penny didn't speak until she sat up to look into the car mirror. "Oh my God," she shrieked, parting her fingers, "look at the blood!"

"Penny … I'm-sor-ry … I-did-n't-want-it … to-go-this-far … please-don't-hate-me!" I began sobbing loudly.

"Come to the washroom with me, Nova," she said to calm me down. "Maybe it's not that bad."

It *was* bad, though.

"Good God, Nova! Look what you've done," she said as she pulled her hands away from her face in front of the washroom mirror. "I really did get to you. Mike, I hope you're worth all this." She tried to laugh it off.

"Why-why-could-n' ... I-jus'-be-hap-py ... for-you? What's-wrong-with-me?"

While I continued to sob, Penny washed the blood from her face. The marks underneath looked like she had met up with a bobcat, which didn't make me feel any better.

"Now wait," she said, "it kind of looks like I walked into a prickle bush. That's what I'll say, that it happened on the way to the washroom in the dark, that I couldn't see without my glasses and walked right into one." She seemed to know my guilt.

Once we were sure the bleeding had stopped, we went back to the car for some sleep.

I was up before Penny, so I joined Flo at the picnic table as she was preparing bacon and eggs for breakfast. First she asked, "Did you sleep well?" and "Were you warm enough?" Then, "How did Penny's date go?" and "Where did they go?" and "What time did she get back to camp?"

I just shrugged my shoulders, but with each question came flashbacks of what had happened only a few hours beforehand.

Soon Penny arrived at the table, looking down to hide her wounds. As I looked sideways at her face, trying to imagine how much it hurt, I wished I could somehow undo the damage I'd done.

Flo didn't notice a thing at first; she was too busy getting food onto plates. It was when she was teasing Penny about being out late on a 'heavy date,' and putting her breakfast in front of her that Flo finally noticed.

She was speechless for a moment and then said, "What the hell happened to you? Did you get into a fight with Mike or something? Couldn't he take 'no' for an answer?"

"No, that's not what happened." Penny began panicking for an explanation. I was afraid she might tell the truth, but she answered, "I fell into some prickles on the way to the washroom. I wasn't wearing my glasses and this is what I got."

I turned to see a suspicious expression cross over Flo's face, as though she found it hard to believe that a stumble into a bush could do so much damage to one face.

"What were you drinking last night that you forgot to put your glasses on? It more looks like you met up with a mountain lion. Do you want some ointment or something?

"No, I think it'll heal faster if I leave it alone. Thanks anyways." Penny looked at me and started eating her breakfast.

I felt relieved that the subject was coming to a close. Still, I worried about what Penny's parents would say.

I couldn't believe Penny's parents' reaction. Mrs. Stanley had a 'what's done is done, nothing we can do about it now' attitude, and Mr. Stanley's reaction was pretty much the same. I suppose I shouldn't have been surprised. Penny's parents were usually too busy with their own activities to care much about her.

During the first few days of grade ten, every second person asked Penny what had happened to her face, and she told the same story over and over: "Well you see, I was walking without my glasses in the dark and.... "

Each time she had to tell this lie, guilt dug deeper into my head. I kept thinking that even Penny's worst enemy wouldn't have done such a thing. At least I had one thing to be thankful for, something no other person would have given: Penny was still talking to me.

CHAPTER 20

ᵒᵉᵗᵒ ᵗᵉᵒ

At seventeen years of age I should have been entering grade twelve, not grade ten, in the fall of 1973 at Selkirk Senior Secondary School, but being behind had a few advantages. Three more years in the school system meant three more years to develop friendships. I also looked forward to three more years of school dances, house parties, ski trips, lake parties and camping trips.

Graduation was an event I wanted and yet didn't want, because I knew that afterwards my social life would take a nosedive. Friends would move away to attend college and university, or to find work. Others would get married and in no time be busy with families.

Out of a fear of the future, I tried to make the most out of any social gathering. I devoted a lot of time and energy to my friends – and because of this, I perhaps cherished bonds of friendship more than they did.

Once classes and school activities were well under way, I gave Penny some breathing room. After having spent so much time together and what had happened between us, I felt she needed a break from me.

For a long time, Penny didn't set foot in our house, and I

seldom went over to her place. My mother always suspected I was responsible for Penny's wounds. She probably thought that Penny wasn't coming around because she hated me for what I had done to her face.

But Penny and I knew differently. All was forgiven. There would always be friendship between us, no matter what.

Time away from Penny led me to a new gang with a few familiar faces. Wayne, Ruby and Karen (an old friend from elementary school) were part of a large group of teens that hung around the pool. Whenever I'd head there for a smoke they'd include me in their circle, even though it seemed to be filled with couples.

Wayne had begun dating Cathy, my old friend from fifth grade. And Karen was dating Frank, a boy who years back used to tease me from behind all the big guys.

It took me a while to get comfortable with this new crowd, and of course it took a while for some of them to get used to me. But I soon figured out who would light a cigarette for me, who would wait up when we were walking, and who really cared whether I was around or not.

There were a couple of times that Penny came up to the pool. I felt bad when the others would give her the cold shoulder, but the fact that she had gone out with Wayne worked against her. They all wanted Wayne and Cathy's relationship to work, so to them Penny was a threat.

After a while, Ruby seemed to take the place of Penny. She became the one to invite me for dinner and tell me about her crushes on guys.

There were quite a few advantages to chumming with Ruby. She lived only a few blocks away, her brother Bob was always nice to me, and she was always ready to listen when I felt miserable about my handicap.

⚬⚬⚬

At Selkirk, the year was divided into semesters. I had four courses for the first half of the year and four new courses in the second half.

One of my courses first semester was Typing 10. My teacher's name was Mr. Caron, well known as a kind and understanding man.

I had also taken typing in grade nine and had been able to raise my speed from ten to twenty-two words per minute. Even though I had improved, I was embarrassed because my classmates ranged from thirty to sixty words per minute.

In an effort to narrow the gap between myself and my classmates, I cheated in Mr. Caron's class. I simply kept my practice tests in my machine and added to them when the actual tests took place.

At first I was nervous doing this. The risk of getting caught was pretty high, but it seemed to work. My average went to thirty-five words per minute, not the highest in the class, but not the lowest either.

A few weeks before our first report card, Mr. Caron walked to the back of the room where I sat. In his hand was a piece of paper. As he came closer I could see that it was the previous day's test. "Nova," he said calmly, "I don't mind if you talk in class or even tell the odd dirty joke, but there's one thing I cannot let my students get away with and that's cheating. Now, I know you have your problems typing, but there's no reason in the world for you to cheat."

Mr. Caron, one of my favourite teachers. He had a
great sense of humour – and was loved by all.

Even though Mr. Caron seemed as kind as everyone said, I thought for sure I'd fail typing for what I had done.

Then he added, "Now, if you'll just relax, take your time and concentrate, you'll do fine. You won't be at the top of the class for speed, but your accuracy will improve. You've been given this special typewriter for a reason. That is to get through school, so take my advice. No more cheating!"

I felt relieved. He could have booted me out of class or yelled at me in front of everyone, but he told me in a reasonable way to cut it out and take my time. I respected 'Mr. C.' for that, and I never attempted to cheat in his class again.

My typing did improve, and by the end of the semester, I could accurately type up to thirty words per minute, and I got a passing grade on my final report card, along with a 'G' for good effort.

The last day of the semester break, some of us from the new gang decided to do a day trip to Radium Hot Springs.

The two-hour drive began slowly because of a fresh snowfall. I rode in Frank's car, along with Karen. Wayne took Cathy in his dad's car, and Randy drove Ruby in his family's car.

I thought Frank would take it nice and easy because of the snow, but I was wrong. Our car led the way and as soon as we hit freshly plowed, dry pavement, things got exciting.

Wayne pulled out and passed us on a straight stretch, and Randy followed. The two of them weren't just passing to get in front; they were drag racing!

"They're not going to leave us in the dust," Frank told Karen as he stepped on the gas. That's when I pulled myself off the back seat to watch the speedometer: seventy, eighty, ninety, one hundred....

Excitement ran through my body as I watched the needle continue to climb, but when it got to the point where it had no farther to go, I hid my head in my jacket.

I heard a muffled scream from Karen, something about black ice, and I could feel the car seeming to float. I dug my head deeper into my jacket, expecting the worst, but nothing happened.

I twisted my head out to see that Frank had simply taken his foot off the gas because we were catching up to the others.

Thankfully, Karen nagged Frank the rest of the way to Radium, and we managed a safe arrival.

It didn't take long for us to put our suits on and get into the hot springs. Wading through this outdoor pool in the middle of winter was strange. The piping hot water and steamy air made it seem as though we were in a gigantic pot that was boiling and ready to overflow.

I wasn't the greatest swimmer, but that didn't matter. The pool was just for sitting in. All of us congregated on a submerged cement bench in the middle. I just sat there, low enough to keep warm but with enough of my head out to feel safe. I joked with the others as they paddled around and dunked their heads into the bubbling water. Through the steam I caught glimpses of the mountains gathered around us. I could see the snow on them sparkling.

It's like a dream, I thought, so I let myself dream. I dreamed the minerals in the hot springs were healing me, taking my CP away, making me normal.

But next thing I knew Wayne was tapping me on the shoulder saying, "Nova, we'd better get going."

We stopped at a roadside diner on the way back to Kimberley, but I didn't want to go in. Even though I was with friends, insecurity took over. In the restaurant there'd be neither water nor steam to conceal my palsied body. I didn't want to embarrass my friends as I staggered in, or appear freakish as I ate.

"I'll-jus'-wait … in-the-car," I told Frank.

Karen knew what was on my mind, but spoke to me like a mother encouraging her child: "You can sit right beside me. If you have any difficulties, I'll be there to help."

I didn't like being talked to that way, but decided not to put up a fight. I slid out of the car and went in with the others.

I preferred sitting in a booth. The place had two, back to back, but they were taken. The counter was the only place all of us could sit together. I grabbed the furthest stool, right next to the wall.

I ordered what everyone else had, a deluxe cheeseburger. I thought that would be the easiest to eat. The bun, however, was on the stale side and crumbled when Karen attempted to place it between my hands. Then the meat squished between my fingers and tomato juice ran down the inside of my arm. I wanted to clean myself up with a napkin, but when I freed my right hand from the mess, my meal fell to the floor.

I told Karen to leave it, and sat for the rest of the time sipping a chocolate milkshake through a straw.

As we left, I looked back to see the messy floor beneath my stool; it was something you'd expect to find under a high chair. I felt my face burning in the icy air as we made our way outside.

I worried about how these new friends felt, and I wondered what they might say behind my back when we got home, maybe: "At times, when Nova eats, it kind of turns my stomach" or "It takes longer to do anything when Nova's around."

It hurt to know they probably said such things, but I also knew I'd feel the same if I was looking at me through their eyes.

The next weekend, I attended a party with the same friends. The guys brought a couple of cases of beer, a bag of pot seemed to appear out of nowhere, there was loud music, the whole bit.

Later, as people were passing out and couples were retreating to corners, a group of us got into a weird conversation. I don't know how it came about, but we started talking about my handicap. They all talked about how hard it must be to cope with. Then they discussed how much they noticed people watching me and how different people teased me.

"There was this guy in our Math class," said Wayne, "and he was making fun of your speech and walking. I stood up for you and told him he didn't know you, and that if he did, he'd see you as a good friend."

That made my mind go back to the times Wayne had been a

creep, such as when he spat at me or, along with certain boys, taunted me.

Those times were in the past. Now he made sure I was included in everything that went on. I had become one of his best friends, and sometimes he and Cathy even asked me for advice.

But talking this way about my handicap made me self-conscious and depressed. I let them know exactly how I felt about being the way I was.

"I-hate .. walk-ing-down ... the-street," I said, breaking down. "Jus'-the-thought ... of-one ... per-son-star-ing ... at-me ... both-ers-me-more ... than-an-y-thing. I-must-have ... made-you-all-sick ... on-the-way-back ... from-Ra-di-um," I added. And the tears cascaded down my cheeks as I recalled my disastrous eating experience in the diner. Before long I had everyone crying along with me.

To prove that they cared, Ruby, Cathy and Karen walked me home, all of us arm in arm. The whole way, they assured me they thought the world of me.

We hugged like sisters in front of my house. They made me feel like I belonged. I was one of them: no better, no worse.

CHAPTER 21

ஒஞ் ஓஒ

I turned eighteen and Ruby turned sixteen the spring of 1974. Like all car crazy teens in Kimberley who turned sixteen, she wanted a learner's license.

I'd been dreaming of driving for two years, but I couldn't convince my Dad to let me apply for a license. Still, he let me practice driving around the ski hill parking lot, and I was pretty successful at it. Once in a while, if there was no traffic, he even allowed me to drive up or down the road leading to North Star Mountain.

Even though he had never criticized my driving, I knew how he felt. My hands weren't steady enough to safely control the steering wheel and my feet didn't react fast enough for the brake and gas pedals.

The day of my eighteenth birthday, I brought up the subject of applying for my learner's license. Dad surprised me by saying, "Meet me in front of City Hall tomorrow after school, and we'll see about that license."

When I called Ruby to share my good news, she said she'd try to talk Tiny into taking her, too.

The next day started off according to plan. Dad arrived at City Hall about ten minutes after me. I could tell by his face, however, that either work had been hell or something else was bothering him. He wasn't in a very talkative mood.

When we got to the licensing office, Ruby and Tiny were already in line, about six people ahead of us. It looked like it would be a long wait, so I tried some small talk. I tried to tell Dad about a few stories we were reading in English class, but his mood showed in his eyes, so I turned my back to him and quietly waited in line.

The line moved so slowly it seemed to be lulling everyone to sleep. Ruby and Tiny were the only ones who seemed wide-awake. They were deep in conversation, pointing to people in the office.

Out of the blue, Dad broke out with, "I've had enough of standing around here like this! Come on, you'll have to do this another time when they're not so busy!"

Before I could say anything, he was out the door. I didn't know whether to leave my place in line or try to call him back, but after standing there stunned for a few seconds I followed, looking briefly back toward Ruby who had heard everything.

"Catch ya' later, Nov'," is all she said.

I waved and plodded away filled with embarrassment, an embarrassment greater than my CP had ever caused.

Dad seemed angry for days, so I forgot about my license for a while. Even after a few weeks, when we were back on speaking terms, talk of a return to the licensing office was taboo.

It wasn't easy listening to Ruby brag about how she had easily passed her learner's test. It was even tougher to see Tiny's car drive by our house regularly as Ruby worked on her driving skills.

Close to summer holidays, I pushed my father to explain.

"Look, Nova," he said in an exasperated tone of voice, "I could sign for you, but how do you know they'll even let you write the test? They might take one look at you, see how much you shake, and say 'No way' in front of all those people. Wouldn't that embarrass you?"

There was some truth in what my Dad said, but I didn't let up. Every couple of days I'd try to bring up the subject. I wanted my chance to write that test. I wanted a chance to drive.

My father never did take me for my learner's license. He inquired about it, but the licensing office needed a certificate from our family doctor stating I had the capabilities and coordination to drive.

When we visited Dr. Lang, he didn't even take time to think about the request. "Nova, I don't think it's a wise thing for you to be driving a car," he said.

When I tried to explain that Dad had already taught me the basics in the ski hill parking lot, he went on to say, "But Nova, what if it was like this? You're just driving along slowly and some guy comes out of nowhere and runs into you. When he sees you shaking the way you do, he'll blame everything on your CP and argue that you shouldn't have been driving a car in the first place. I think it's better if you forget the whole thing."

I respected Dr. Lang, so I reluctantly tried to take his advice to heart. I never brought the subject up again with my father. I knew I'd hear, "What did Dr. Lang say?"

My dream of driving was on hold.

๛๑๏ ๑๏๛

I got through my first year of senior high school with average marks.

My parents praised me endlessly for passing to grade eleven. This wasn't hard to understand. If I made it successfully through grade twelve, I'd actually be their first child to graduate! Since Jeannie had been robbed of her chance and Flo and Nita had chosen the family route, my graduation would be as much *their* proudest moment as mine.

As summer got under way, my mother decided it was time for me to get a job, and I agreed.

Spending the holidays babysitting for Flo and Nita wasn't getting me anywhere. I needed to start making a decent wage. A job would also give me a chance to get my self-confidence up and prove to myself I could earn my keep.

Finding employment for a disabled person, however, is not easy. CP is a huge handicap in the eyes of an employer. Most people wouldn't even let me babysit because they were afraid I'd break some precious household item or, worse yet, have a spasm and drop a child.

So, Mom took me down to the Human Resources office and explained my situation. When they weren't very receptive, she got pretty nasty, saying, "How can you give money to people who are perfectly capable of working but don't, and not help my daughter find a job? She wants to work!"

A few days later, Human Resources called with a job offer. If I was interested, I could receive training as a playground leader. I'd work with small children, organizing games and crafts, as well as supervising other fun activities.

The trouble was that, ever since I could remember, little kids were the worst for making fun of me. I understood their reactions (to them I must have seemed retarded or just plain weird), but still it hurt to be laughed at or teased.

Nevertheless, I accepted. In a matter of days I was packing

for a weeklong training camp in Fernie, which is about 130 kilometres east of Kimberley.

I was frightened to death as my parents drove me there because I found out that over fifty other teenagers and young adults from the eastern part of the province would attend. I worried about how these strangers would treat me as I talked, walked and ate with them.

I also wondered whether the people who'd be teaching me would know about my CP. I hoped Human Resources had sent a letter explaining that there'd be things I couldn't do as well as the others.

When I arrived at the training camp I was relieved to see a few familiar faces from Kimberley – kids from school and others I recognized from around town.

And camp wasn't as bad as I thought it would be. As I went through the week, learning arts, crafts and playground games, I made friends who seemed to see right past my handicap.

Even meals weren't that bad. I just picked foods that were easy to stab with a fork and made sure I had my drinking straw.

On the last day, after all the dishes had been cleared away in the mess hall, there was a little going away ceremony. Each person received an award, a certificate for passing the course.

Our instructors handed out certificates in alphabetical order. A few people went up before Bannatyne was called, each one receiving polite applause. When my name was called, I hesitated. I was a little afraid to take my turn in case I tripped or ripped the paper away, tearing it in two. But I had come too far not to finish the week properly, so I mustered the courage to stand. Then I walked as steadily as I could to the instructor who'd called my name, gave a smile, shook his hand and grasped the certificate carefully with my right hand. I turned around and stopped dead. Everyone was standing, and they began clapping and whistling and yelling things like, "Way to go, Nova!" When I got back to my seat, a group of people surrounded me and began slapping and patting my back.

Being a playground leader was fairly simple. Every Monday morning there was a staff meeting in the Kimberley Civic Centre boardroom. Our supervisor, an athletic guy named John MacKenzie, designated two people for every playground. Each person was given a whistle, a key to open equipment lockers and a jacket for identification.

My first assignment was the park nearest my own neighbourhood. This suited me fine, because most of the children would know me.

After a few weeks on the job, my fears of how the kids were going to react to my spastic body disappeared. I soon found out that more than anything else preschoolers care about one-on-one attention, so I always made an effort to get to know each child. As long as I accepted and liked them, they accepted and liked me.

I can tell you, what they did and said gave me a lot of laughs. They had the funniest ideas about my condition. One boy said I was so unsteady because I had a wooden leg. And one little girl said I must have eaten the wrong kind of vitamins to be walking so weirdly.

I got to know children from all over Kimberley. A few who didn't know any better still teased me, but I won the trust of most others.

The kids I was closest to encouraged me to do things I was usually afraid of or too embarrassed to do because of my handicap. For example, they talked me into trying the trampoline.

Luckily, my partner the day of this challenge volunteered to go on the trampoline with me. His name was Richard; he was over six feet tall and had a reputation as a great athlete.

With someone to hang on to, especially someone who knew what he was doing, I looked pretty good up there.

But more importantly, I got over my fear of the trampoline.

For the rest of the summer I surprised many an onlooker by always taking a turn on the trampoline.

I got to really enjoy the feeling of bouncing up and down, and I used to fantasize I was an Olympic gymnast training for competition.

It took me back to when I was little. I'd jump on my bed and pretend I was something special, that I could outdo anybody. Whenever Mom caught me she'd break my train of thought by yelling at me, just like the kids in the playground would do when my five minutes were up.

I was sad when my final week of work came around, but things were busy enough to keep me from becoming depressed. The entire playground staff had to work overtime to plan a carnival in McDougall Park for youngsters from all over Kimberley.

Along with arts and crafts, we prepared relay races and other competitive games. Fortune telling gypsies and a haunted house were on our agenda, too.

I ended up running the haunted house and asked Ruby to help. Dressed as an ogre, I led the kids through after Ruby had blindfolded them. I made them feel buckets of spaghetti meant to be monsters' brains and made them crawl through cardboard box tunnels so we could make spooky noises from above.

"I-never-would've-thought … that-work-ing-for … mon-ey … was-going-to-be … so-much … fun," I said to Ruby later as we headed to the Grill Café for some supper.

CHAPTER 22

O nce school got under way I didn't see as much of Ruby. She was a year ahead of me, and since graduation was foremost on her mind, she stuck pretty close to her grade twelve friends.

The rest of my friends, the gang that hung around the pool, had gone their separate ways: Cathy and Wayne broke up, Karen moved to Vancouver to find an office job, and Frank and Randy left Kimberley to find work, too.

Penny, on the other hand, was in my English 11 class, and after a few weeks we were the best of buddies again.

Penny had developed her own circle of friends in the previous year, including a very likable girl named Nancy. It didn't take long for me to find out that Nancy wasn't well; she had contracted multiple sclerosis (MS) at the start of grade eleven.

At first I joked about having another handicapped person in the school, but then I realized how different Nancy's condition was from CP. When I found out how many pills she had to take and how many doctors she had to see, I felt kind of lucky.

Penny sat in the desk right in front of me in English. We'd discuss the books we were reading and partner up for some assignments. Normally two chatty girls would be separated, but we had a very modern and understanding teacher.

Mr. Rosen was a thin man in his middle thirties. He stood about six-two, had a dark beard and hair that reached his shirt collar. Of the adults Penny and I knew, he was one of the few who looked positively upon our generation.

Like with all my teachers, I was a little shy about having to use my electric typewriter instead of writing with a pen or pencil. But Mr. Rosen was pretty open-minded. It didn't bother him at all if I tapped away noisily in his classroom.

Mr. Rosen seemed to understand and accept my quirks and needs better than my other grade eleven teachers. He had seen me working with his little girl during the summer, and maybe that had something to do with it.

My Social Studies teacher, Mr. Murphy, was another tall, bearded man with a unique style of teaching. In his class there was hardly any written work. We'd read about world events in magazines like *Time* and have long and lively discussions. I can actually say that I learned more this way than by reading text-books and doing reports.

One person who really got under my skin, however, was the Girls' Counselor. Unexpectedly, I was called to her office one day. At first I thought she was going to give me a lecture about my schoolwork, but I couldn't understand why. The little home-work I had, I did, and none of my teachers seemed displeased with my progress. She reminded me of my junior high school Girls' Counselor – kind of high class with snobby airs about her. But she seemed even phonier, and I am sure that any girl in the school would have described her the same way.

Nobody knew exactly how tall this lady was. Her four-inch

heels made her taller than any of the male teachers, and her hairpiece added what seemed another two feet. She had a horsey face, so her head looked kind of like a unicorn's from a distance. Sitting across from her, however, all one saw was a lady in her middle fifties with gobs of make-up, false eyelashes and fingernails that seemed half as long as her long skinny fingers.

"Well, Nova," she began, "I guess you're puzzled about why you were pulled out of class just to come and see me, eh?" Her voice, as usual, sounded a little phony, but because she was my superior I mustered up a respectful reply.

"Yes-ma'm ... but-get-ting-out ... of-Eng-lish ... is-n't-so-bad ... you-can't-do-that ... ev-ry-day." I chuckled as I spoke, and she chuckled back.

"I call in all of the girls in your grade to discuss their future plans," she went on. "I thought this would be a good time to get to know you better and see what you want for the future." Her kindness seemed too good to be true.

As we started talking about the courses I could take in grade twelve, her tone of voice changed. Instead of helping me plan a schedule, she focused on how difficult each subject would be.

"With a handicap like yours and having to type all your work, you'll experience a lot of difficulties next year," she said, before changing the topic to my career plans. "What kind of work do you want to get into, Nova?"

"Well-I ... would-n't-mind ... work-ing-with-kids ... or-may-be ... soc-ial-work," I answered, feeling flustered.

She smiled. "You know, I'll bet if I talked to someone down at Human Resources, we could get you into a job right now. Then you wouldn't have to struggle next year trying to keep up with the others to graduate."

I couldn't believe what this woman was suggesting. Ever since I had entered the regular school system, I had dreamed of graduating. And even though I was two steps behind everyone else my age, I still wanted graduation! No one in my family, including my parents, had ever graduated. Also, I'd be the only student from Mrs. Baglot's special class to finish grade twelve and receive a diploma. Nobody was going to deprive me of that special moment.

"Are-you-tell-ing-me ... my-grades ... are-n't-good-e-nough?" I looked straight into her eyes.

"No, Nova, your grades are a little above average. If you can keep them there, your chances are very good. I'm just saying that the work isn't going to get any easier. Maybe you'd like to avoid the pressures of grade twelve and start working as soon as possible. After all, you're going to turn nineteen soon. You'll be the oldest student in the school next year. If you fail, it might be embarrassing."

"I-would-like to take ... that-chance ... if you don't-mind. I-have just ... as-much-right to make it ... to-that ... fin-ish line as ... any-body else, right?"

She nodded her head.

"There's-no-way ... you can ... force-me-to-leave school ... is-there?" I was getting cocky without meaning to.

"I wasn't trying to say it that way," she said, changing her tone and playing up to me. "But it's going to be rough. If you think you can keep those grades up above average, I admire your courage and wish you all the luck."

"Ya-thanks," I said as I let myself out of her office.

When I told my friends and family what the counselor had said, most of them were furious. My mother was ready to report her to the school board. My father, however, had his own opinions.

"She was probably just thinking of your welfare, Nova," he said. "Now, the thing you have to do is prove her wrong. Get good marks and make it to the top if you can. Come the day you graduate, you can look her in the eyes and smile."

Dad made a lot of sense: the best thing to do was prove the woman wrong, nothing more. So from then on I continued to get my homework done, and whenever there was a test, even a small one, I studied hard.

Not long into the New Year, Penny began to excite me with romantic talk about a new boyfriend, Neil. He was from a small village north of Kimberley. Neil was nothing like the man I had always pictured for Penny. He was short, not tall, and fair-haired, not dark.

At first I was shy around him because I wanted him to notice as little of my handicap as possible. But Penny took the time to explain my physical condition, and before long we felt pretty relaxed around one another.

I tried not to be envious of the new love in Penny's life. But it was hard to be unattached while they were together. I hadn't had a sexual experience, and yet I thought about sex constantly: *What would it be like with a man I loved? What would it be like with a man I liked? What would it be like right now – with anybody?*

I thought back to my babysitting days in Lethbridge. A neighbour of Flo and Stewart's used to visit me regularly. My first summer there he told me I had a nice body. The second summer he wanted to make love to me. I was tempted but turned him down. As I watched Penny and Neil's relationship heat up,

I wished more than once I'd been weaker and gotten lucky in Lethbridge!

After about a month together, Penny and Neil's relationship ground to a halt. I couldn't believe it. Just as I was getting used to the guy, he was out of the picture. It really bothered me to see Penny's pain after that break up. If she heard a love song on the radio or if someone in her family mentioned Neil, she'd be in tears.

What broke the two up was a mystery, and for a while Penny couldn't talk about it. She was an excellent student and her work was always printed out so neatly it made my typing look messy. But shortly after breaking up with Neil, her work seemed to take a turn for the worse. Her health changed, too. I thought it was psychological and missing Neil was making her sick. Then I suspected it was some sort of flu. After a visit to her family doctor, Penny finally confided in me.

She told me as we sat on her parent's basement couch. She lit a cigarette first, with her hands shaking so much I thought the doctor must have discovered some deadly disease. I didn't know whether to cry right away or wait until Penny confirmed my way of thinking.

"Nova, I'm pregnant," she said, her troubled eyes looking right into my mine as the words came out.

I didn't know how to react to this news. I sure felt stupid for not realizing sooner what her problem was. "How-do-you feel ... about-the ... sit-ua-tion?"

"I'm confused and I'm not sure what I should do. Mom knows. I'd like to run away before Dad gets home, but there's no way she'll let me out of the house."

"Hey-Pen' ... are-you go-ing ... to-get in-touch-with Neil ... and let-him know?"

Penny finished the rest of her smoke before answering, "I don't know what to do."

About a week after Penny told me her news, she dropped out of school.

When we next met, for dinner with her family, her spirits had brightened, which surprised me. She then informed me that after a heavy meeting with Neil and both sets of parents, everyone had agreed that they should get married. This news caught me completely off guard.

"Real-ly? You're-gonna ... mar-ry Neil! Con-grat-u-lations!" I was truly happy for Penny. After so much heartbreak, she was going to have a future, a home and most important of all, Neil.

After dinner, everyone began discussing plans. The wedding would be in May, just both families and a few close friends. I didn't have to ask whether I'd be a guest; I knew that one way or another I'd be there with bells on my toes, but once again Penny threw me off guard.

"You'll be my one and only bridesmaid, won't you, Nov'? I know a big church service would make you self-conscious, but the ceremony will be right here in the house. How about it?"

She wanted an answer right then and there with her whole family looking at me, so what could I say?

"I'll-be glad to ... but-I-might trip ... coming-in-to the room ... or-knock ... the-bride and groom ov-er ... in-the mid-dle of ... their-vows," I joked.

Everyone assured me they had faith I'd pull it off.

Penny's wedding took place on the tenth of May 1975.

The bridesmaid's dress I wore was my first formal gown. I

had ordered it from the Sears catalogue. It was light blue with little white daisies and the neckline dipped so what bust I had showed just enough. Mom had also bought me some white gloves to cover my heavily scarred, unfeminine hands.

Penny wore a scarlet gown with white trim, long sleeves and a high collar.

With a private ceremony, it didn't really matter if we coordinated. Furthermore, we had decided it was more important to get dresses we liked and could wear again.

The two of us got dressed in Penny's bedroom, a place where we'd had some of the wildest conversations, more than a few arguments and a couple of good cries. I knew it was the last time we'd be together in that room. After the wedding, I'd be visiting her in a mobile home north of Kimberley.

A temporary pulpit was set up in the living room and the guests formed a semi-circle behind it. Neil and his brother, Ivar, stood opposite the minister as Penny and I entered. Getting into place was a breeze. Not once did I slobber or stumble or drop my bouquet. But, when the time came for everyone to stand still during the opening prayer, my CP got into the act.

The flowers in my bouquet began to vibrate like the tail feathers of a peacock. I tried holding the bouquet in a different position, but there was no way my hands were going to relax. Even worse, sweat from my forehead ran down the side of my face. Soon my face was the colour of Penny's dress.

As Penny and Neil exchanged vows, Penny's dad came to my rescue, by gently placing his hand under my elbow. This didn't totally calm the shaking, but it was enough to keep my flowers from flying and helped me concentrate until the final "I do."

It would have been too embarrassing for me sign the register,

Matron of Honour at Neil and Penny's wedding. Ivar
(on the left) was best man. My bouquet was shaking
throughout the service.

so Penny had her future sister-in-law sign for me. At first I felt
excluded, like I was missing a crucial part of the ceremony. But
the clicking and flashing of cameras that followed, catching every move the four of us in the wedding party made, eased my
disappointment. I was Penny's maid of honour, no doubt about it!

Next was the reception, which was open to dozens of family
members and friends who hadn't attended the service. On the
way there, Penny and Neil presented me with a slender black
velvet box; inside was a silver identification bracelet inscribed
with NOVA. Not being good at expressing emotion, all I could
do was look at the gift, then look at them.

"It's your bridesmaid's gift," said Penny. "It isn't very much, but I knew you always wanted one."

"Thank-you … ver-y-much … it's beau-ti-ful," I murmured before teasing, "now-when some-one … asks-me my-name … and-I-for-get … I can look-at-my-wrist."

"Are you sure you know where your wrist is?" Neil joked back. He was feeling pretty happy about everything that was happening on that warm Saturday in May.

Before we reached the reception hall, I gave them each a short hug and kiss to show I really did appreciate the bracelet.

All eyes were upon Penny, Neil, Ivar and I as we stepped through the doors of the hall. Ivar led me slowly to the head table and pulled my chair out so that I could be seated. This was one of the first times that a gentleman had treated me like a lady.

As I sat down and got a good look at the people who filled the hall, it didn't take me long to decide that I wasn't going to eat much. There was no way I was going to let my shaky hands fling food around the head table at a wedding reception.

Once the formalities were over and the dancing started, I began to feel just like any other lonesome person at a ball. Neil and Penny took off, Ivar danced and socialized with his wife, and everyone else celebrated around me.

I was surprised that Penny had invited Ruby. Like me, she was sitting alone, but at the back of the hall. I ambled over to ask her how she was enjoying the evening. We soon got into a discussion about the ceremony, and she had a good laugh when I told her how my bouquet had nearly shaken apart.

Later, after a few drinks, Ruby gave me a lift home.

CHAPTER 23

⋰ↄᴑᵉ ᵉᴑↄ⋱

I saw a lot more of Ruby after Penny's marriage. Our friendship got back on solid ground for a few months.

But then she started hanging around with a girl named Susie, a petite, pretty blonde who had her own car. As the school year wound down, the two of them drove regularly to nearby Cranbrook to cruise for guys, but they'd never ask me along.

Once, after I put up a fuss and made Ruby feel guilty, they did take me. But whenever a car full of guys tried to pull up beside us, Susie took off on them. I was pretty sure that she didn't want them to look inside the car and see me.

I best remember the evening that Ruby phoned and said she needed a break from Susie. She ended the conversation by saying, "Come on over. We can look for something to do downtown."

When I arrived at her place, however, she'd gone out with Susie after all. Ruby's thoughtlessness pissed me off, and one evening I somehow got it into my head to hide in a field near her house. *It's not that cold*, I thought. *I'll just have a smoke and wait. Wait for what?* I didn't know, but still I sat in that field from nine-thirty until after midnight.

As I sat there, I wondered if Ruby's neighbours could see me and suspected a weirdo or thief was lurking in the grass. Nobody confronted me and my patience paid off. At about twenty after twelve, Susie's car pulled into Ruby's driveway. I pressed my body into the ground to make sure that the two of them couldn't see me, but I was all ears.

"Thanks a lot, see ya'," I heard Ruby say before Susie's car pulled away. Then I heard her heading for the front door.

I couldn't stop myself from yelling out: "Hey-Ruby!" I was on my feet trying to act like I was coming from somewhere else by the time she spotted me. "Where-have … you-been?" I asked, trying not to sound like a nosy parent. "You-asked … me-over, remember?"

"Just driving around," was her curt reply. "Why are you hanging around so late? There's school tomorrow, ya' know. What are you anyways, a spy or what?"

"I-couldn't sleep … just-went for a walk … go-ahead, hand-cuff … me," I held out my shaky hands, trying to be funny.

"Changing my mind isn't a crime, either," she snapped. "What's with you? Are you keeping tabs on me every time I'm out?"

"Hey … if-you-don't … want me-around, just-say-so. I-guess … this-cripple isn't welcome … around-here anymore. I can take-a-hint."

"Get off it with that self pity BS. I just found something better to do than sit on the lawn smoking. If Susie doesn't ask you to come, there's not much I can do, is there?" She was upset but kept her voice low because people in the house were asleep.

"Why-don't … you like-me anymore, Rube? Is-it … my handicap? You're-my best … friend … I-don't want-to lose you," I pleaded, unaware I'd begun to cry.

"Shshsh! You'll wake up the whole house," she said almost comfortingly, her anger gone. "I can't stand here talking. I have to get some sleep. You go home and I'll see you in the morning, okay? Good night."

See you in the morning. She wouldn't have said that if she didn't want me around, I thought, and my sobbing subsided.

As she closed the door, I said, "Night-Rube," and I headed for home.

But things didn't change much between Ruby and I – except I didn't wait outside her house anymore. I'd phone her a lot more than she'd phone me, sometimes every hour if she was out. Those calls sure got on Tiny's nerves! As time went on, I became even more obsessed with Ruby. I guess the fear of losing her friendship began to overpower me.

Mom noticed a change in me. Sometimes she'd hear me arguing with Ruby on the phone and later find me crying in my room.

One day she sat on my bed and said, "Why don't you let Ruby go? It's obvious she thinks she's too good for you now. You've got lots of friends and you can certainly get along without her."

The next day, as I walked to school with Ruby, I told her what my mother had said, hoping to make her feel guilty. But the more I talked, the angrier she became. "You're the one ruining what friendship we have left," she accused me. "You're acting like a child who needs someone to hold her hand all the time."

When graduation time arrived, Ruby was even more distant. Along with her regular trips to Cranbrook with Susie, she was busy with grad parties and preparations.

I could accept that someone in grade twelve couldn't be bothered hanging around with someone in grade eleven during this hectic time, but it was her exclusion of me in favour of Susie that hurt most. Still, to my surprise, she sent me an invitation to the graduation ceremonies.

On the evening of Ruby's grad, Tiny invited me over. I remember giving Ruby a rock record and a card that said something about being friends forever. Then, after a few kind words were exchanged, we were all off to the Kimberley Civic Centre for the ceremonies.

As Ruby and the rest of the graduates marched onto the cement floor of the facility to take their seats, I realized that I was hopefully only a year away from the same experience. *Will Ruby be in the bleachers looking excitedly down upon me?* I wondered.

After the passing out of diplomas, a few entertaining stories and the valedictorian's address, five scholarships were handed out. Of course those who were expected to receive one did, but the fifth name called was Ruby's.

This was a great surprise to me, and even more of a surprise to her family. I could see tears in Tiny's eyes as Ruby went up to accept the award.

There were many toasts for Ruby back at her house after the ceremony, but the celebrations soon went sour for me when Susie pulled up in her father's car. She and Ruby were heading off to Wasa Lake for the grad party, the biggest party of the year.

And, as usual, I was not invited.

⚬⚬⚬

By the time grade eleven came to a close, I had finally accepted the fact that I needed to find someone else to hang around with, or at least find something else to keep myself occupied.

Our local Human Resources office came through for me. I was hired under a provincial government grant called Careers

'75. All I was told at first was that I'd be involved in a project that would benefit handicapped people.

My first day of work was mostly an introduction. I found out about the job and became acquainted with my co-workers.

My boss and the head of our project was Douglas Munn, a blind man from Victoria. In his late forties, he was tall, thin and walked aided by a white cane. He amazed me because he could talk like a professor, smoke filter-less cigarettes and read people's minds all at once.

Linda, his assistant, was another blind person. She was from Kimberley and I had seen her around before, usually walking arm in arm with someone else. I had never before realized that she was blind and being guided.

I soon found out that I'd be working closely with three other girls: one able-bodied, one deaf and one with arthritis.

I sat quietly as Douglas Munn related the details of our job. He explained how we'd be examining buildings in the East Kootenay region to determine their accessibility for people with disabilities.

It took a while to become comfortable with my co-workers.

Maryanne, the able-bodied person, was a tall, husky girl. She was a university student whose summer home was Cranbrook. She was big but she was a pushover, one of those people who do anything they're told. Still, the fact that she was studying to be a teacher gave me a complex.

How can I measure up to someone so smart? I thought.

Jeanette was the deaf girl. To look at her, you'd never know that she had any kind of disability. She had a speech impediment, but her brown curly hair and slim figure made her handicap seem pretty insignificant. I'd have put any money down on a bet that she had no boy trouble.

Then there was Marcy. With her arthritis, she walked a bit slowly and had problems reaching for objects. However, she was wholesome looking and sweet, like a friendly next-door neighbour. I also found out that her cousin was a classmate of mine. So in the early part of the job, I quickly grew to know Marcy.

On our first real day of work, Douglas introduced us to the tools of our trade.

There was a level to measure the slope of the walkways used for accessing buildings. There was also a strange looking scale that hooked onto doors to measure their resistance. And, of course we had a measuring tape to measure the area of washroom cubicles and the heights of door knobs, toilet paper dispensers, light switches, and so on.

The job seemed like it was going to be a piece of cake. But, of course, we also had to keep records, and that was out for me. I solved this by ensuring that I had a partner all the time, someone to do the recording.

Our trial runs took place in downtown Kimberley. At first I was embarrassed because of the way people reacted. Some of the storekeepers would look at us oddly or ask humiliating questions like: "Who hired you for such a stupid job?"

But as soon as we informed them that we were the official reps of the provincial government, they were more cooperative.

It took us three weeks to inspect all the necessary buildings in Kimberley. Then we moved on to Cranbrook.

Outside of work, the summer also went better than I'd anticipated.

I even went out a few times with Ruby and Susie, until they

started dating a couple of boys, which knocked me out of the picture again. But instead of sitting around moping, I found other things to do.

For one thing, I'd visit Penny and her baby, Nicole. It was too far to walk to her place, but occasionally I'd catch a ride with my father or hitchhike there.

When the baby was sleeping, we'd watch TV, gossip and talk about old times.

One time I confided in her about Ruby and Susie's treatment of me because I didn't know if I had any right to feel rejected.

Penny's advice was, "Stay away from them, and avoid the hurt."

There were other nights when I'd meet up with old friends from elementary school. Marcy's cousin and I went back as far as grade four. She had an apartment above a downtown store that made a great partying spot.

On just about any summer night, that one-bedroom apartment was filled with girls. If I walked around town long enough, I'd inevitably run into someone who was heading there and willing to invite me along.

I loved having a summer job, and in time I grew quite close to my fellow workers. After all, when you work side by side and eat lunch with the same people five days a week, you can't help but get to know them.

In Cranbrook we usually ate lunch in a downtown park that was filled with office workers. Late in August, during one of our lunches together, a young man who looked very familiar came walking our way. It took me a few seconds to recognize Cliff, my next-door neighbour's cousin. He said hello to me and asked if he could join us.

Cliff was slim and tall. He had blond hair and sad blue eyes, but when he smiled it somehow improved his expression. As the final weeks of my summer job went by, he joined us regularly for lunch. He talked mostly with me, which didn't seem to bother the others. We discussed everything from rock music to politics.

Before long I had a crush on Cliff, and I know Maryanne, Jeanette and Marcy knew how I felt.

On the Monday of our last week, they seemed to purposely leave Cliff and I alone, excusing themselves to the other side of the park.

He watched them walk away, and then said, "That Jeanette is very pretty...."

I felt a rock hit me inside.

But to my surprise he quickly turned to say, "...and I think you're pretty, too. Let's meet at the water fountain tomorrow."

With my emotions skyrocketing, I replied, "Yes ... let's."

It seemed the next day took forever to come.

And then, when I arrived at work Tuesday morning, I couldn't believe my rotten luck. We were sent to a small town outside Cranbrook for the whole day.

My first romantic rendezvous, and I stand the guy up, I thought miserably as we ate lunch in a greasy restaurant.

And things got worse. My final three days of work were too rainy to attract man or beast to the park for lunch, so there was no way of telling Cliff what had happened. Furthermore, I was too embarrassed to phone him.

On our final day, there were tears between Maryanne, Jeanette, Marcy and me. I cried the hardest, and I think they knew why.

꧁ ꧂

CHAPTER 24

꧁ ꧂

My final year of high school got off to a lonely start. All of my closest friends had graduated already, dropped out of Selkirk or moved away from town.

Like always, the first day of school was a day when everyone wore their brand new outfits, renewed old friendships and told wild stories about their summer vacations. Though I hadn't travelled anywhere exotic or experienced a fulfilling romance, working had been the highlight of my summer, so mostly I talked about that.

My final year of high school also got off to a confusing start. I couldn't help analyzing my situation: *Who was I? I was a handicapped nineteen-year-old student trying to fit in with able-bodied sixteen and seventeen-year-olds. My cerebral palsy? I wasn't sure I could continue to handle it. Sometimes it wasn't a big thing, but always present was the reality that it was going to stay with me for the rest of my life. Could I cope? I'd be soon facing the world outside school, so I'd have to. If I couldn't accept my handicap, how could I expect anyone else to?*

Soon after school started, Ruby telephoned to tell me she'd found a job at Mary's Kitchen, a local restaurant. With that call our friendship was on again, but in a much more casual way. We seldom bickered, and I even got to know and like Susie thanks to a few "girls' nights" out.

One of my best friends at school was a girl in Mr. Caron's Office Orientation class named Coral. I had seen her around for years but had never really gotten to know her.

Coral was your average blonde-haired, blue-eyed Miss Popularity, someone who I'd always assumed would never give me the time of day. The only thing I could see we had in common was grad in June. We both liked joking around in class though, and a friendship seemed to blossom out of nowhere.

Coral was in school to pick up one more course for graduation. After the first semester she was a free woman! Still, that didn't end our friendship. Sometimes we'd meet for lunch, or I'd tag along around town with Coral and her boyfriend, David.

I missed Coral in the second semester, but I didn't react as I had with Ruby. I didn't become possessive out of fear of losing her friendship, and I wasn't jealous of her and David.

Parking with Coral and David was a bit of a problem, though. It was hard finding something to do while they were preoccupied. It was even worse when they brought along David's friend, Kenny, and his girlfriend. The two couples would invariably start necking, which left me forgotten. I had no choice but to stare into space and maybe sip on a bottle of beer.

Once, when Kenny was sitting between his girlfriend and me in the back of David's Camaro, I started cracking everybody up with one joke after another. Kenny must have thought I was pretty lonesome or something, because he grabbed me and started sucking on my neck. When his girlfriend pulled him away everyone noticed a huge hickey below my right ear. Kenny's girlfriend and David took it as a joke, although Coral thought it was a bit ignorant. As for me, I was determined to make the most of it.

Having a hickey on my neck for the first time was only a little bit embarrassing. For a girl who'd never been out on a date, I liked how it made people wonder. When kids at school asked me questions, I'd just roll my eyes and keep them in suspense. Making them believe I had a secret mystery man was good for my image.

Ruby, who didn't really know Coral and her friends, almost went crazy trying to figure out who the guy was. Kenny's hickey didn't come at a good time as far as my parents were concerned, however. They didn't care enough to even ask where it came from, but they did care that it was going to ruin a photo session they had pre-booked for the whole family in Lethbridge.

I can tell you, that was one family portrait I showed off to everybody I knew!

⊱⊰

Even though every school day had its frustrations and challenges, I was determined to enjoy my final year. Two teachers who helped me keep my spirits up were Mr. Caron and Mrs. Dellert, the teacher for my Child Care course.

I can remember one particular class with Mr. Caron that had the whole class in stitches. We were practicing telephone etiquette, and a conversation between us went like this:

"No-va's Pi-zza-ria, may-I ... help-you?"

"Yes, I was wondering if I could have a pizza delivered to my home?"

"Sure, what-kind ... would-you ... like?"

"Well, I'll have a medium cheese with chopped rubber boot and a small pepperoni with hot mustard and soap shavings."

"Are-you-sure … that-you … would-n't like-a-large … crab-grass and pond-muck special? I'll-even throw-in … a-pint-of pond-water … to-help-you wash-it down."

"Why not! And throw in the kitchen sink, too!"

"All-right-sure! Give … the-delivery-boy … a tip-for-me, eh?"

In one of Mrs. Dellert's last classes, we had a guest speaker on disadvantaged children. It was the one and only Mrs. Baglot! Her daughter and son, Lorri and Jim, were in the same class. I wasn't surprised that, as she got going, her presentation swung around to me.

She touched on the fun our class had, all the boys I chased and kissed, the jokes I came up with, the typewriter that turned my life around, and how she got me to have confidence in myself. She helped my classmates realize how difficult it was for me to reach grade twelve.

By the end, Mrs. Baglot was in tears as she expressed how proud she was that I'd be graduating. I was in tears, too.

If I hadn't yet received a heaven-sent lift in life, I got one that day. Mrs. Baglot reminded me how I had knocked down any obstacle that got in my way, and she helped my peers see me in a new light. But most importantly, she let me know, even without saying so, that I always had a friend in her.

After Mrs. Baglot's visit, Mrs. Dellert had us write an essay on one type of special needs child. It was to be presented orally in class. She encouraged me to write about cerebral palsy, and I did – even though, the way I looked at it, just because I had CP didn't mean I was an expert on the topic.

My teacher, Mrs. Dellert, encouraged me to write an essay about C.P., and read it to my classmates.

When I gave my speech, I began with the dictionary definition of my condition: "Cerebral palsy is ... a-form-of ... paraly-sis ... caused by brain in-jury ... during-or-before birth ... char-ac-ter-ized by ... diff-icul-ty in con-trol ... of-the volun-tary muscles." I then put the notes aside and talked straight from my heart.

I talked about going to Children's Hospital for therapy, being misunderstood, and getting teased, all the while knowing and trying to convince others that I was just as good as any other human being.

My presentation must have been a moving one for my classmates because many of them complimented me on it afterwards, and more than a few did so with tears in their eyes.

೪ᏇᏂᏭᎦ

In Mrs. Dellert's class I got close to two girls, Linda and Marge. Toward the end of March, each of us talked our parents into paying for a plane ticket to Vancouver for spring break.

As I packed for the trip, I can remember praying that the city with so many terrible childhood memories would finally bring me some excitement, and maybe even some romance. Linda and Marge's parents arranged for them to stay with relatives, so my father took the liberty of arranging for me to stay with my Auntie Laura.

When I arrived at my aunt's, I soon realized not much had changed since I was a kid. The way she *wanted* me to be and the way I *was* were two different things.

I hated how she treated me like a prisoner. I was capable enough to make my own decisions, but I had to fight for permission to do anything. Furthermore, she'd interrogate my friends before we headed out on the town, making them feel like it was their responsibility to babysit me. She seemed to take great delight in my embarrassment.

On the positive side, while I was there my Uncle Bobby dropped by for a visit. He still told jokes, but he wasn't nearly so playful as he had been when I was little. In fact, the years had turned him more moody than playful. He was extremely sensitive to anything that was said. Yet, compared to my aunt, or any other relative for that matter, he was still number one.

The highlight for me on that trip was meeting up with Jackie, my first love from Mrs. Baglot's class. I knew he lived in Vancouver, so Linda, Marge and I arranged to meet him for a movie. We chose *One Flew Over the Cuckoo's Nest*, which I thought was appropriate considering the way I had acted around Ruby.

As we waited for Jackie in the lobby of a downtown theatre, like a love-starved fool, I started imagining falling in love with him all over again. He ended up arriving a little late, but that didn't matter because when he walked into the well-lit lobby, it was like a thousand more lights went on.

Of course, Jackie was no longer the boy I had kissed secretly in elementary school. He still had the same baby-blue eyes, but he was now a young man with a manufacturing job in the big city. He was single and lived in his own apartment.

He's come a long way since leaving Kimberley, I thought as we gave each other a quick hug.

After the movie, as Jackie drove us home, he and I entertained Linda and Marge with stories about the crazy stunts we pulled off in Mrs. Baglot's class. We seemed to cover everything but us, and so I got the feeling that he didn't want to remember holding me in his arms and kissing me.

Jackie drove me home last, but there would be no romance that evening. After another quick hug, away he sped, leaving me standing alone in front of my aunt's apartment building.

Linda, Marge and I became closer friends after our trip to Vancouver. We talked about our adventures and the sights and opportunities there for weeks. We decided that, compared to Vancouver, life in Kimberley was painfully dull.

Cranbrook wasn't Vancouver, but for a change of pace Linda would sometimes drive us there in her father's car. One night before heading back to Kimberley, we grabbed a snack at a drive-in. Linda parked across from a car full of guys that we flirted with. They ended up inviting us to a party in a nearby apartment.

I was a bit hesitant to go, because they were strangers, and I also feared they might get carried away and start teasing me.

As it turned out, they were pretty understanding. One of them in particular, a tall redhead named Scott, was very friendly.

Before long, to the enjoyment of everyone else, he and I were trading dirty jokes. Then he got carried away, but not by putting me down. He started tickling me, to see how much I could handle.

Unfortunately, by the time Scott and I were well acquainted, it was very late and time to head back to Kimberley. As I said good night to him, I was filled with sad thoughts. I knew the chances of ever seeing him again were likely one in ten thousand.

Since the previous summer I had secretly hoped I'd meet a special fellow who could be my grad escort.

So far, I can remember thinking as we drove home, *I've struck out three times: Cliff, Jackie and Scott.*

ﾟⓞℓℓ ℥ℰℓﾟ

In the final months of grade twelve, I didn't give up hope that I'd find an escort for grad. Ironically, my graduation fantasies became focused on the unlikeliest of dates for me, someone in my Community Recreation class named Bruce.

This was a guy I had hated in junior high school. Back then, every time he saw me in the hall he'd stiffen his body, walk like Frankenstein, and pretend he had food in his hand. Saying, "EAYT! EAYT!" he'd smack the food against his forehead, making every kid in sight laugh. Oh, how I'd hated the guy!

But Bruce had changed. He'd say hello in the halls and in Community Recreation class he'd help me during activities like curling and bowling. After school he was often there to help me

*Bruce and I at a party. Because I was two years older
than other graduating students, I could legally drink.*

light up a smoke, and since we were both nineteen, we even went
out for a beer. In every class, it seemed he sat close by, and we
got along so well that by the end of the year I couldn't help but
get my hopes up for graduation night.

But as it turned out, Bruce had a love life after all: a long
distance romance with a girl in Cranbrook. By June he'd shared
a few details, and I knew that this former enemy had become
another fantasy, forever no more than a friend.

In the final weeks of school, Bruce would ask me about my
love life. I'm sure he was sensing that I was desperate for a date.
Unfortunately, I had nothing to tell him, right up until grad.

⚬ᴏ☯ ☯ᴏ⚬

Our graduation ceremony was held at the Kimberley Civic Centre. The day I'd waited so long for had finally arrived!

On Graduation Day, the excitement that had filled the halls of Selkirk for months peaked. One hundred and twenty graduates, lined up alphabetically, filed into the Civic Centre, not sure what to expect. Ahead of me walked Lorri and Jim Baglot.

I sat down, scanning the stands desperately, searching for my family. If I could find them, I knew they could see me. It didn't take long before we spotted one another. I noticed that close to them sat Mrs. Baglot with her husband. She had recently told me that she was proud her "three kids" were graduating.

The graduation ceremony was like others I had been to, a little boring until the person you were there for was on stage. Wearing one of the prettiest gowns out of the Eaton's catalogue, a gift from my parents, I waited for my name to be announced.

My sky-blue satin dress cascaded around the chair I sat upon, but I waited with an empty feeling inside. I was embarrassed to be experiencing grad without an escort; I thought, *Out of 75 girls, I'm the only one without a date.*

My CP embarrasses me, too, but it's a part of who I am. I found peace in this thought and proceeded to think about my accomplishments.

I looked again at my family, sitting so proudly in their seats. When I did, I thought about Jeannie: *She would be proud of me, too, if she could be here....*

Before long the principal was reading my name: "Nova Bannatyne!" My sisters, parents and the thousand or so people in the arena were on their feet, saluting me with a standing ovation.

*I rise to receive my diploma in the prettiest dress
I had ever worn. Graduating from high school
was the proudest moment of my life.*

Cover photo: *Me at age 4 in my "... ugly, high army-like boots." Not long after this I met Ellen Baglot, and she changed my life forever.*

AFTERWORD

by Ellen Baglot

With apprehension on my first day of employment as a teacher aide, I faced children with physical and mental challenges. I secretly asked myself: "What am I doing here?" Looking around at those who were having difficulties in moving, seeing, hearing, thinking, I was left wondering what I could possibly do that would make a difference. Then, I knew. Those two deep brown beautiful eyes and that instant beckoning smile – NOVA! She was looking up at me and magnetically drawing me into her life. Neither of us would ever be the same as our eyes met. We both knew there was magic there. She summoned me to come inside, look beyond what others saw as a disability and discover the person and potential inside. At the same time, she was passing

227

that reciprocal message back to me. Those eyes said to me, "I know I can do it, I'll try anything, just give me a chance!"

Things have not changed. Nova continues to reach out and share the essence of who she is, this time sharing her personal story and proving yet again that she "can do anything!"

In her story, Nova does not dwell on her difficulties in walking, using her hands, speaking, swallowing or balancing. Instead, she lets us see how she is more like others than she is different. We also experience the angst of all children as they learn to be accepted by others and be held in real friendships. We are compelled to think how much more life must be intensified to not let a disability get in the way of a true relationship. So often, acquaintances for those who face disabilities are arranged, contrived, or paid for. Not for Nova. She wanted to be, to do, and to belong like everyone else. Moreover, she never used her difficulties as an excuse, whether it was to type, paint a picture, ride a bike, play hockey, or, later in life, drive a car, get married, give birth, or drink a glass of wine. She did it all.

As we absorb her story, we are sometimes lulled into thinking that all things can be overcome by someone as bright, determined and humorous as Nova. Then she provides insight into those times when friends excluded her, perhaps thinking, "Nova can't do it" or "It might embarrass Nova or others if she's included." It was hard for her close friends to explain, and at times they hid their feelings. Nova knew. Our hearts break, but then we realize that occasionally there are differences in all of us that must be endured. Nova lives with this every day. Yet, as painful as that may be, she has learned to use laughter, humour and forgiveness to overcome.

Nova and I have travelled a long road together, and her

achievement here in sharing her story signifies so much of that relationship. She learned from me and I most certainly learned from her all along the way. Our lives have been intertwined her whole school and adult life. My life and many others' lives are richer for that.

In the beginning of the 1960s, our world had not become aware of human equality in practice and barely in consciousness. Mainstreaming was not happening in society. Nova was therefore pioneer-like in her efforts to be included amongst those children whom she would call "The Normals," and the small supportive community of Kimberley allowed this to happen. Still, few in society at large were exposed to the outward physical appearances of people with challenges; they were often segregated because they were so different, and therefore little thought was given to the emotions, feelings and dreams behind those differences. Nova's fight to make others aware of her right to belong was her mission in life. She accepted it wholeheartedly and shares it with us until the last word of her introspective story.

After graduation, Nova left Kimberley for the big city. It is important to note that when she arrived in Vancouver at the end of the 1970s, no students like her were integrated in any of the schools, never mind looking to belong in the adult world. This was her next challenge. She sought the help of Jack Webster, well known radio celebrity, when she was denied employment and residency because she was physically different. And once again, as an advocate and example, she awakened in others the understanding that each belongs by questioning, "Why not?" She challenged barriers and many were removed. Nova went on to become a wife, mother, and contributing citizen, and so this story was just the beginning of her remarkable journey.

Just think, Nova could have been normal, though she leaves us doubting that. Even without the effects of cerebral palsy, our Nova would never have settled for 'normal.' She was and always will be extraordinary – and for that we love her!

~ Ellen Baglot, Nova's first teacher, forever a friend

AN EPILOGUE IN PICTURES

NOVA BANNATYNE
N.N.: "Skunk"
AMB.: Day care
supervisor
P.P.: People who
walk too fast
F.S.: "You're
lucky! "

1976 – I graduated from Selkirk Senior Secondary School, Kimberley, British Columbia, on June 7th, 1976. Here is a photo of my Grade 12 graduation class and my high school yearbook write-up.

1977 – After experiencing discrimination while looking for work in Vancouver, I sought help from CJOR radio talk show host Jack Webster and appeared on his 'City Mike' radio show. Soon after, I was hired temporarily by the Downtown Eastside Residents Association on a short-term grant. Later, I secured a full-time position with the Greater Vancouver Regional District as a mail clerk – all thanks to Jack!

1979 – When Jack Webster moved from radio to television, I was one of the first guests to appear on 'Webster,' his talk show on BCTV. The top photo of us was taken at a party celebrating his move to television.

2000 – Ray and I paid a surprise visit to Jack during the taping of his last Webster show. (Lower photo)

1978 – I acquired my driver's license and bought my first car, a Ford Zephyr station wagon. Here I am with my pride and joy.

1980 – I met Ray Eng through a co-worker and we married on August 9th, 1980. Here is a photo of us on our wedding day. Ray and I pose between my parents, Garnet and Cherry Bannatyne.

1980 – I was a very happy bride with my yellow roses.
Ray and my mother, Cherry, were always good friends.

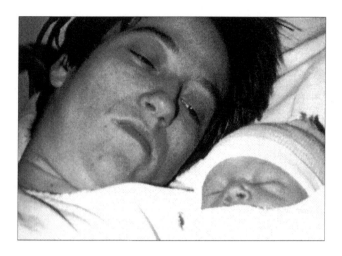

1981 – Our daughter Jamie was born on October 16th, 1981.
1986 – Ray and I welcomed our son Jackson into the world
on March 28th, 1986. Here is a photo of Jamie with her baby
brother. I was so proud of my babies – still am!

1989 – Ray took this photo of Jackson, Jamie and me at the Vancouver Game Farm.
1990 – Ray and I with Jackson in our living room in Surrey. Ray, who worked as a custodian for the Surrey School District, was a loving husband and devoted father.

1999 – This is Jackson's Grade 8 school photo.

2004 – Our last family picture before Ray's passing away of a heart attack in 2007. Jamie is 23 and Jackson 18 years old.

*2010 – Jamie and I at the Olympic Women's Hockey Game.
Yeah! We won!*

2011 – My high school friend Bruce Gilmar poses with me and Jamie (29 and now married), on January 23, 2011, during my mother's memorial service in Kimberley. Bruce was the guy in high school who, before we were friends, would tease me mercilessly. He would "... stiffen his body, walk like Frankenstein, and ... saying, EAYT! EAYT! ... smack food against his forehead, making every kid in sight laugh." I hated him then, but he became – and still is – one of my best friends. The lower photo of young Bruce appeared in our Yearbook.

2013 – Here is Ellen Baglot between her daughter Lorri and me. My "second mother," who – since the death of my own mother – I now call "Mum," resides in suburban Vancouver and we visit one another often.

ACKNOWLEDGEMENTS

I would like to thank all the people who supported me during my formative years, as well as those who have worked hard on my behalf to help this book come together. Especially, I thank my family, Jack Webster (deceased) and all the teachers who demonstrated devotion and unconditional care for me – and in particular, Ellen Baglot, who wrote the *Afterword*, and Gladys Legget (deceased), who supported my move into the public school system. I also thank my childhood and high school friends for their support, along with a special mention to Kevin Smith, who helped me come up with the title, *Just Think, I Could Have Been Normal*. Thanks also go out to Sally Kruse (deceased) and her daughter, Terri, who encouraged me to seek Jack Webster's help and who made me swear I would one day share my story. More recently, Carole Kruse and Bonnie Bonfonti provided invaluable proofreading and editing suggestions.

Further, I would like to thank and acknowledge Richard A. Watson, who gave me permission to use his poem, *Prisoner of Dependence*. Richard was a friend of mine while I was living in Vancouver; his determined spirit and literary genius inspired me to persevere as I composed the first draft of this book.

Finally, I thank my cousin, editor and friend, George Kruse, for helping to make the publication of my story about growing up with CP a reality.

ABOUT THE AUTHOR

NOVA BANNATYNE-ENG

Nova was born with cerebral palsy in Kimberley, BC, on April 14, 1956. Currently she lives in Surrey, BC with her cat, Oliver. Her husband Ray Eng died of a heart attack in 2007 at 61 years of age. Her grown children – daughter Jamie and son Jackson – live close by, and Nova is a loving grandma to Jamie's son, Andrew.

Nova worked in housekeeping for the Centre for Child Development in Surrey, B.C. until February 2013. She has spoken to school children and other special interest groups about the challenges of living with cerebral palsy, and she plans to expand her role as a presenter and advocate in the future.

Made in the USA
San Bernardino, CA
22 June 2020